"Timothy Paul Jone... ...mpelling, and often humorous. He captivates me with everything he writes. When I read his writing, I have many 'Aha!' or 'I wish I'd thought of that' moments. *Finding God in a Galaxy Far, Far Away* is not the first great book that Timothy has written. And it won't be the last. Make sure you don't miss reading it!"

DR. JIM GARLOW
SENIOR PASTOR, SKYLINE WESLEYAN CHURCH
SAN DIEGO, CALIFORNIA

"Timothy Paul Jones has a knack for finding Christian parallels within the *Star Wars* universe and then showing readers how to apply these truths to their lives. If you own a lightsaber—or a Bible—you're sure to benefit from reading his book."

KEVIN MILLER, AUTHOR AND REVIEWER
HOLLYWOODJESUS.COM

"'Awe-some' reading that both delights and challenges us. Timothy Paul Jones blends personal narrative with moments from film that touch upon our common journey of faith. A fun and thoughtful book for Christians who consider and enjoy popular culture and media."

ROBERT W. PAZMIÑO
VALERIA STONE PROFESSOR OF CHRISTIAN EDUCATION,
ANDOVER NEWTON THEOLOGICAL SCHOOL

"The Force is strong with this one. *Finding God* is an insightful journey connecting the fictional *Star Wars* universe and real-life faith. It is full of thoughtful insights that will deepen your life and help you better understand why God created us and how He intended for us to live. I could not recommend it more."

JOSHUA GRIFFIN
EDITOR/OWNER, THEFORCE.NET
MANAGER, PURPOSE DRIVEN YOUTH MINISTRY

FINDING GOD IN A GALAXY FAR, FAR AWAY

TIMOTHY PAUL JONES

Multnomah® Publishers *Sisters, Oregon*

FINDING GOD IN A GALAXY FAR, FAR AWAY
published by Multnomah Publishers, Inc.

© 2005 by Timothy Paul Jones
International Standard Book Number: 1-59052-577-9

Cover image of car by Stephen Gardner, PixelWorksStudio.net
Author photo courtesy of Vicki Albright.

Unless otherwise indicated, Scripture quotations are from:
The Holy Bible, New International Version
© 1973, 1984 by International Bible Society,
used by permission of Zondervan Publishing House

Other Scripture quotations are from:
New American Standard Bible (NASB) © 1960, 1977, 1995
by the Lockman Foundation. Used by permission.
The Message © 1993, 1994, 1995, 1996, 2000, 2001, 2002
Used by permission of NavPress Publishing Group
The Holy Bible, New Life Version (NLV) © 1969, Christian Literature International.
The Holy Bible, English Standard Version (ESV)
© 2001 by Crossway Bibles, a division of Good News Publishers.
Used by permission. All rights reserved.

Multnomah is a trademark of Multnomah Publishers, Inc.,
and is registered in the U.S. Patent and Trademark Office.
The colophon is a trademark of Multnomah Publishers, Inc.

Printed in the United States of America

For information:
MULTNOMAH PUBLISHERS, INC.
601 N. LARCH ST.
SISTERS, OREGON 97759

Library of Congress Cataloging-in-Publication Data
Jones, Timothy P. (Timothy Paul)
  Finding God in a galaxy far, far away / Timothy Paul Jones.
    p. cm.
  Includes bibliographical references.
  ISBN 1-59052-577-9
  1. Spirituality. 2. Star wars (Motion picture) I. Title.
  BV4501.3.J662 2005
  242—dc22

                                          2005017000

05 06 07 08 09 10—10 9 8 7 6 5 4 3 2 1 0

For my big sister, Shyre.
Remember when I drew Luke Skywalker on your term paper
before you turned it in?
And when I chattered about *Star Wars* until your ears ached?
This book is what I was trying to say then,
but didn't know how until now.
Thanks for listening.
You lit up my life.

THE PHANTOM CONTENTS

Part III
"Impossible to See, the Future Is"
Experiencing Awe in the Unexpected

A Long Time Ago, Not Far from Here...

A long time ago in a galaxy far, far away...

OPENING LINE OF EACH *STAR WARS* FILM

This book's genesis can be traced to a drive-in theater in southern Missouri, nearly thirty years ago. I was only five years old when I took my first steps into the *Star Wars* galaxy, but I decided then and there that I would someday write about this epic space opera.

The early drafts were not promising—they consisted primarily of crayon and ink-pen portrayals of Luke Skywalker and Han Solo. These sketches appeared on pretty much any piece of paper I could find around the house, including my older sister's junior term paper.

In the years following, I became fluent in more sophisticated forms of communication—not quite six million, mind you, but I *did* learn how to pull a few books together. So as the release of *Star Wars: Episode III—Revenge of the Sith* approached, my longings to write a book on this subject were revived, along with my penchant for throwing a fit in the aisle of Wal-Mart when I'm not allowed to purchase my favorite action figure.

Special thanks to David Webb and the fine folk at Multnomah Publishers for their work on this manuscript. Thanks to my most magnificent friends Deby Nottingham and Laura Franklin for their comments on the early drafts of the book—each of you is quite clever, for a human being. Thanks also to the members of First Baptist Church of Rolling Hills who graciously granted me a flexible schedule to complete this book and who patiently listened to several of these chapters in the form of Bible studies and sermons.

Finding God in a Galaxy Far, Far Away was written at Panera Bread Company on Forty-first Street in Tulsa, Oklahoma, and at Mojo's Famous Bar-B-Q on Historic Route 66 in Catoosa, Oklahoma. Thanks to the staff at both restaurants for fueling this project with copious quantities of Asiago cheese bagels and bar-becued hot links.

Finally, for their tireless patience while I worked on this book, my wife, Rayann, and daughter, Hannah, deserve more thanks than I can possibly express in a single manuscript. Like the sun and moon, the two of you fill my life with light every day and every night. You are the most precious gifts that God has given to me, and I stand in awe of the glory I see in you.

If it's been awhile since you watched the *Star Wars* movies, you may want to read the appendix, "A Whirlwind Guide to the *Star Wars* Saga," before proceeding. Otherwise, begin with chapter 1—and may the Force be with you!

Timothy Paul Jones

Every Journey Has a First Step

Every generation has a legend.
Every saga has a beginning.
Every journey has a first step.

TRAILER FOR *STAR WARS: EPISODE I—THE PHANTOM MENACE*

We have come from God…[so] inevitably the myths woven by us,
though they contain error, reflect a splintered fragment of the true
light, the eternal truth that is with God. [1]

J. R. R. TOLKIEN

A sluggish breeze meanders down the northern footings of the Ozark Mountains, barely rustling the scrubby walnuts and stately pines. The wind whispers through the jagged rows of automobiles gathered in the graveled lot, but the occupants do not hear its voice. They are waiting for the time-between-the-times, for the mystical moment when the last shimmers of sunlight wither from the western sky. In that moment, the rhythmic stutter of the film projector behind them will begin, and the white panel before them—now nothing more than a towering wall of cracking wood and peeling white paint—will become their window into a larger world. Many of them already know the words that will herald the genesis of their journey.

A long time ago in a galaxy far, far away…

No one has anticipated this moment with more zeal than a certain five-year-old boy, seated in the third row of vehicles. Well, perhaps "seated" isn't quite the right word. The backseat of his parents' Ford Pinto gave up on containing the boy's ecstasy nearly an hour ago, quietly resigning itself to being prematurely frayed by a perpetually squiggling posterior. The Dr. Pepper—clasped in a cup in his hands—has not helped.

The boy is here to see a space adventure. Starfighters and battle stations, spaceships and blaster guns—these are the plot components that have compelled this child to plead with his parents for this moment. What he does not know is that he is about to experience more than a space opera; his perception of reality is about to undergo exponential expansion. For here, in this least likely of places, he will, for the first time, experience *awe.*

At last, twilight enshrouds the drive-in theater in shadows. Even through the tiny speaker that dangles above the Pinto's dashboard, the movie's initial fanfare heralds the advent of something extraordinary. It is John the Baptist bellowing in the Judean desert, Paul Revere plunging through the brick alleys of Boston, the Beatles cranking out the opening chords of "I Saw Her Standing There." It is an announcement that the world is about to change.

The separation between sky and screen is no longer discernible. It is as if the stars from a galaxy far, far away have become the native stars of *this* sky, strewn across *this* horizon. The opening text is not projected upon a screen; it is flung upon the firmament.

The boy cannot read all of the words that crawl from the bottom of the screen and vanish into the distance. But he is aware that there is a vastness depicted here that he has never known, a cosmic conflict beyond what he has ever imagined. And it is not far away; it is here, in this place.

For the first time, the boy is experiencing *awe*.

By the time the Imperial Star Destroyer roars over the roof of the little Pinto, hot on the trail of a Rebel blockade runner, the child is transfixed, seized by this sense of awe—so transfixed, in fact, that his cup of Dr. Pepper slips from his hands. The carpet of that 1977 Ford Pinto was probably never the same after that night.

But then again, neither was I.

Is "the Force" the same as God? No. Even George Lucas has said, "I would hesitate to call 'the Force' God."[2] God, as described in the Scriptures, is a personal, spiritual being, capable of receiving love and worship (see Deuteronomy 6:4–9; John 4:24). The Force of *Star Wars* is an impersonal energy. Even so, the concept of the Force in *Star Wars* pulls together universal themes of sacrifice, self-denial, and infinite mystery—themes that flow from the longing for eternity that is present in every human heart.

The Universal Yearning

Although I couldn't put it into words at the time, I discovered a vital truth in the backseat of that Pinto: *I was created with a longing for awe.*

So were you.

According to the Scriptures, "[God] has...set eternity in the hearts of men" (Ecclesiastes 3:11). Another translation puts it this way: "He has put thoughts of the forever in man's mind" (NLV). There is, in every one of us, a longing to touch "the forever," to sense the magnitude of the vastness in which we live.[3] This awareness may occasionally include fear, but fear alone cannot satisfy our souls' deepest longings. What each of us craves is that mystical moment in which our amazement at all that stands beyond us unites in passionate embrace with our fear of all that is still lacking within us.

The religious researcher Rudolf Otto referred to this inner hunger as a longing for *mysterium fascinans et tremendum*—for the "mystery that fascinates and yet terrifies."[4] William James described it as a yearning for the state of mind "in which the will to assert ourselves and hold our own has been displaced by a willingness to close our mouths and be as nothing in the floods and waterspouts of God."[5] Put in simpler terms, every human soul desperately desires to experience *awe*.[6]

This universal longing explains why we ride roller coasters, tell scary stories, and gaze into the Grand Canyon's gaping expanse. In each of these experiences, our awareness of our own smallness in a vast and mysterious cosmos rubs shoulders with sheer amazement.[7] This universal longing for awe also explains why, after nearly thirty years, the popularity of the *Star Wars* saga shows no sign of subsiding. Somehow, these twin trilogies have conveyed to millions of viewers a sense of awe—and it isn't only the spectacle of the films' opening seconds that conveys this sense.

At the heart of George Lucas's space opera is a world that is full of wonders. An invisible Force binds the universe together, and an impetuous farm boy is able to tap into its power. An undersized green alien with backward syntax and bushy ears is the wisest warrior of them all. And deep within the villain's sinister armor is a grown-up child who aches for his mother and whose dying wish is to see his son with his own eyes.

In a world that is glutted with glitz, gorged with superficial pleasures, and yet starving for authentic awe, sagas of this sort stimulate the imagination anew. These stories seize the space in every human soul that still longs to see exceptional beauty and power in the most improbable places. They stir our latent longings for awe—just like our favorite stories from the Bible.

Remember the story of Moses? Wandering through a barren wilderness, the hot-tempered shepherd watched a desert bush erupt with the fire of God, and his life was never the same again (see Exodus 3). Remember Isaiah? Walking into the temple, the prophet heard the song of the seraphs and, suddenly, found himself flat on his face before the splendor of pure holiness (see Isaiah 6). How about Peter, James, and John? Three fishermen scrambled up a hill, following their teacher, and saw the flesh of a Galilean carpenter transformed into blazing light, terrifying in its intensity (see Mark 9). In each instance, the spectators found themselves amazed at the immensity of all that was beyond them and yet frightened by their own shortcomings. They experienced *awe*.

> *The most beautiful and most profound emotion we can experience is the sensation of the mystical... The one to whom this emotion is a stranger, who can no longer wonder and stand rapt in awe, is as good as dead.*[8]
> ALBERT EINSTEIN

> awe *n.* The point at which our amazement at the immensity of all that is beyond us and our fear of our own smallness unite in passionate embrace.

Learning to Live in Awe

Contemporary people have, however, missed a vital truth about awe: God created us not only to *long for* awe but also to *live in* awe. There's a phrase in the ancient Hebrew that captures the outlook that God expects from us: "Stand in awe" (Psalm 22:23, NASB; see also Psalm 33:8; 65:8; 119:120). In other words, *live with an attitude of awe.* This expectation persisted even after Jesus arrived on Earth. In the presence of Jesus, all sorts of people—publicans and Pharisees, centurions and slaves—were "filled with awe" (Matthew 27:54; Luke 5:17–26). "Do not become proud," the apostle Paul charged the Romans, "but stand in awe" (Romans 11:20, ESV). The author of Hebrews echoed Paul's command, calling his hearers to serve God "with reverence and awe" (Hebrews 12:28). Perhaps most important of all is the clause that the physician Luke selected to characterize the earliest congregation of believers: "Everyone kept feeling a sense of awe" (Acts 2:43, NASB).

Do you see the pattern? Awe isn't supposed to be a sporadic feeling that we acknowledge from a distance, reflected on a screen of silver or recorded in the pages of Scripture. *God longs to weave awe into the daily fabric of our lives.*

In light of this divine longing, I suppose it disturbs me somewhat that the first place I experienced awe was not in a church sanctuary or in a Sunday school class but at a drive-in theater. I had witnessed *excitement* in the community of faith. I had felt *love*. I had even sensed *guilt*. But never before had I experienced this immense impression of my own minuteness within an immeasurably vast cosmos. I had felt much in church that might compel me to walk down the aisle during an invitation, but I had never felt anything that could cause me to drop my Dr. Pepper.

So how can contemporary believers learn to live in awe? More to the point, how do we learn to experience awe not only in the shadow of a mere movie but also in the presence of the God from whose fingertips this wonder-filled world has fallen? The answer is simple—not *easy*, mind you, but simple.

We must learn to see that nothing in our lives is ordinary.

That's it.

Yes, really.

Every aspect of your life is permeated with the presence and the plan of an extraordinary God; therefore, nothing in your life is ordinary. "In him," the apostle Paul proclaimed to the citizens of Athens, "we live and move and have our being" (Acts 17:28). Did you catch that? Every aspect of your life is "in him"—in God. If every aspect of your life occurs in God, there are no ordinary people in your life, there is no ordinary time, and there are no ordinary events. Everything in your life is *extraordinary*. Even the events that happen over and over—sunrises and sunsets, for instance—are not monotonous matters. They are extraordinary affairs. G. K. Chesterton put it this way:

> [Suppose that] the sun rises regularly because he never gets tired of rising. His routine might be due, not to a lifelessness, but to a rush of life… A child kicks his legs rhythmically through excess, not absence, of life. Because children have abounding vitality, because they are in

spirit fierce and free…they want things repeated and unchanged. They always say, "Do it again"; and the grown-up person does it again until he is nearly dead, for grown-up people are not strong enough to exult in monotony. But perhaps God is strong enough to exult in monotony. It is possible that God says every morning, "Do it again" to the sun; and every evening, "Do it again" to the moon. It may not be automatic necessity that makes all daisies alike; it may be that God makes every daisy separately, but has never got tired of making them. It may be that He has the eternal appetite of infancy… The repetition in Nature may not be a mere recurrence; it may be a theatrical encore.[9]

Living as If Everything Is Extraordinary

When I live as if everything in my life is extraordinary, I recognize that the blueness of the sky this morning is no mere meteorological fluke. The sky is blue today because God is wild about the color blue, and at some point in eternity past, God lovingly crafted this specific shade of blue for this specific sky on this specific day.

When I remember that everything in my life is extraordinary, my daughter's unrelenting giggle in the backseat of my car is no annoyance. Hannah's laughter is an echo from eternity, a reflection of the very joy of God, and she is a gift from heaven itself.

When I remember that everything in my life is extraordinary, I discern the goodness of God in the yeasty aroma of a well-baked bagel, in the soft sweetness of my wife's skin, even in the few moments of silence that descend upon me when I find myself gridlocked in morning traffic. When I recognize that there are no ordinary events, my soul is able to sense the halo along the edge of every earthly thing. Then, and only then, do I find myself able to *live in awe*.

That's why the earliest followers of Jesus "kept feeling a sense of awe." They didn't look for God's presence only in the "wonders and miraculous signs." They also embraced the presence of God in events as apparently monotonous as eating, drinking, and simply being together (Acts 2:43–46).

That's why David could compose psalms that were so suffused with awe. He noticed the presence of an extraordinary God in earth and sky, dusk and dawn, storm and sea—even in silence:

> Silence is praise to you,
> Zion-Dwelling God…
> Earth-Tamer, Ocean-Pourer,
> Mountain-Maker, Hill-Dresser,
> Muzzler of sea storm
>   and wave crash,
> of mobs in noisy riot—
> Far and wide they'll come to a stop,
> they'll stare in awe, in wonder.
> Dawn and dusk take turns
> calling, "Come and worship"…
> Creation was made for this!
> (Psalm 65:1, 5–9, *The Message*)

The kingdom of God is not some marbleized Jerusalem we build 'out there' somewhere. The kingdom of God is among us, around us, and within us. Look at the world of a flower. Look at a loaf of bread. Life's magic, miracle, passion, and promise are gifts that fall right in our laps and find their way right into our hands.[10]
LEONARD SWEET

That's also why the *Star Wars* saga has provoked a sense of awe in millions of viewers: Over and over, creatures that seem to be ordinary turn out to be extraordinary participants in this sweeping epic. A Corellian pirate named Han Solo and a farm boy known as Luke, a slave-child called Anakin and even the bothersome Gungan named Jar-Jar Binks…all of them seem ordinary—even less than ordinary—at first. Yet each of them plays a vital role in the redemption of a fallen galaxy.

> *All happenings,*
> *great and small,*
> *are parables*
> *whereby God*
> *speaks. The art*
> *of life is to get*
> *the message.*[11]
> MALCOLM MUGGERIDGE

Awe becomes possible only when we recognize that nothing in our lives is ordinary. Every person and every event that seems ordinary is simply a signpost pointing to an extraordinary possibility. "Luminous beings are we," Yoda informs Luke during the young Jedi's training, "not this crude matter." Our lives are, in other words, far more than movements of flesh and blood that others see. Even when we fail to sense it, we are engulfed in wonder. We are "fearfully and wonderfully made" (Psalm 139:14), and our lives are extraordinary events.

A Splintered Fragment of the True Light

I do not pretend that George Lucas intended his trilogies to lead anyone into a life of divine awe. When asked about the theological aspects of *Star Wars*, Lucas replied:

I see *Star Wars* as taking all the issues that religion represents and trying to distill them down into a more modern and easily accessible construct... I put the Force into the movie in order to try to awaken a certain kind of spirituality in young people... I wanted to make it so that young people would begin to ask questions about the mystery.[12]

Yet in a world where God's extraordinary presence fills even the most ordinary aspects of life, whenever persons begin "to ask questions about the mystery," their stories tend to stumble across some truth—maybe incomplete, maybe misconstrued, but truth nonetheless. J. R. R. Tolkien, author of *The Lord of the Rings* trilogy, put it this way: "We have come from God...[so] inevitably the myths woven by us, though they contain error, reflect a splintered fragment of the true light, the eternal truth that is with God. Myths may be misguided, but they steer however shakily toward the true harbor."

You know the timeless tales that Tolkien was talking about: tales of Jason and the golden fleece, of the Holy Grail and King Arthur, of Belle and the hideous Beast, of the four children who stumbled through a wardrobe into Narnia's enchanted wood, of two plucky hobbits whose determination to destroy the One Ring led to the downfall of the dark lord, and a host of other myths that will be told and retold throughout time because they do indeed "reflect a splintered fragment of the true light."

There is a common thread that ties these timeless tales together: Ordinary creatures embrace extraordinary quests and, in the midst of their quests, it becomes clear that these creatures may not have been quite as ordinary as they seemed. And the readers of these tales? They find themselves filled with awe, for they have recognized—if only for a moment— that, deep inside, they too may be extraordinary creatures. A splintered fragment of true light has pricked their souls.

The *Star Wars* trilogies do not provoke awe because of their stunning cinematography or the astonishing special effects. They certainly do not provoke awe because of flawless casting or faultless scripts. No, the *Star Wars* saga is awe-inspiring because it stands in the timeless tradition of tales that are saturated with fragments of the true light.

The Quest for Awe

I have not written this book from the perspective of a professional theologian. So if you picked up this book hoping for a tedious theological treatise, prepare yourself to be disappointed. I have certainly not written this text from the perspective of a film critic or moviemaker. So if you are looking for salacious behind-the-scenes details from the *Star Wars* films, these pages probably won't satisfy you either.

The perspective from which I've written this book is that of an impatient little boy in the backseat of a Ford Pinto. Oh, he's grown several years older since that night and, once in a while, he's even a bit wiser. But he caught a glimpse of awe in that movie, and it set him on a quest that still continues today. This book is his attempt to share one portion of his quest with you.

The goal for the quest is simply this—to find the fragments of light in the *Star Wars* saga and to see in each fragment a reflection of "the eternal truth that is with God." As we embrace the unique contours of each fragment, may you sense the extraordinary in the midst of the ordinary, the magnificent in the midst of the mundane, the hidden halo along the edge of every earthly event.

Before our quest reaches its conclusion, I hope that you discover something else too: Every instance of awe in this world is merely a distant reflection of the Source of Awe, of the True Light whose glory is too vast to be captured on a DVD and too dazzling to be projected through celluloid. This Force is not an energy-field; He is the one whose fingers first formed energy. This Force is not formless power; He is a personal being and, in a manger in Bethlehem, it was this Force that "became flesh and made his dwelling among us" (John 1:14).

Let the Quest Begin

Well, the previews are over now; it's time for the featured presentation. So raid the fridge for something to drink and toss some popcorn in the microwave. Slide your favorite *Star Wars* movie into the DVD player, and sit back in your most comfortable chair. Then turn the page, relax, and let the quest begin!

Oh, and don't drop your Dr. Pepper.

Why are people who analyze and study Star Wars called loser-geeks with no life while people who analyze and study Shakespeare are called educated scholars? And don't tell me to get a life, or I'll tell you to get an imagination.

ANONYMOUS POSTING ON STARWARS.COM FORUM

Padawan *n.* In the *Star Wars* saga, someone who has been designated the disciple of a Jedi Master.

> # Learn to Live in Awe...
>
> ...by remembering that everything in your life is extraordinary.

SPIRITUAL EXERCISES FOR THE SERIOUS PADAWAN

Be Mindful of the True Force

Plan a day to begin your quest to live in awe. At the beginning of the day, study Psalm 65:5–13. Notice how the psalmist views ordinary events as signs of God's extraordinary power. List the ordinary tasks that you will undertake today—driving to work, running errands, doing chores, even mopping the kitchen floor. Pray about each task, specifically asking God to help you to sense His presence in each one. Locate an appropriate song to mark the beginning of your quest—perhaps "When Will I Ever Learn to Live in God?" by Van Morrison or "Meant to Live" by Switchfoot.

At the end of the day, review your list. Ask yourself, *How did my desire to look for God's presence in each apparently ordinary task help me to see that nothing in my life is ordinary?* Locate a song of praise that focuses on the awe of God. Listen carefully to the song's lyrics as you reread Psalm 65 and meditate on the awe-inspiring presence of God in every aspect of your life.

Meditate on the True Force

My Master and my God,
I wanted my life to be extraordinary.
Yet I must confess…
I thought the only way
    to have a remarkable life
    was through my own efforts.
But my efforts have made me
    miserable,
    irritable,
    everything but remarkable.

Help me to see that a remarkable life
    is not a goal that I can achieve—
it is a gift that I simply receive
    by recognizing that You have
    already made my life an
    extraordinary event.
Teach me to live in awe
    by teaching me to live in You.

PART
ONE

"YOUR FIRST STEP INTO A LARGER WORLD"

Finding Awe in the Present Moment

"ALL HIS LIFE has he looked away…to the future, to the horizon. Never his mind on where he was…what he was doing." That's how Jedi Master Yoda summarizes Luke Skywalker's approach to life. More often than I care to admit, those same words could apply to me.

I dream about the spring and miss the beauty of winter. I envision houses that I might own in the future and miss the joy of the home that God has provided here and now. I fantasize about future vacations, full of blazing sunrises and sandy beaches, and fail to see the simple beauty that surrounds me in this present moment—the cardinal in the evergreen trilling romantic ditties to his sweetheart; the pine tree gently trembling in the breeze; the friends whose lives have fluttered into my path like autumn leaves at precisely the moment I needed them most.

Be Mindful

I don't think I'm alone in my dilemma. As a culture, we have embraced Luke Skywalker's approach to life—looking constantly to the future, to the horizon, to the next new thing. In the process, we completely miss the infinite joy of each present moment. In such a culture:

> We no longer catch our breath at the sight of a rainbow or the scent of a rose… We no longer run our fingers through water, no longer shout at the stars or make faces at the moon… Certainly, the new can amaze us: a space shuttle, the latest computer game, the softest diaper. Till tomorrow, till the new becomes old, till yesterday's wonder is discarded or taken for granted.[1]

So what's the solution? There's a simple instruction the Jedi Masters repeat throughout the two trilogies that comprise the *Star Wars* saga: "Be mindful." In other words, "Be careful what passes through your mind. Make certain that your mind is filled with the peace that is available to you in every present moment." It's good advice, even in our own galaxy.

The apostle Paul made much the same point in his letter to the Philippians: "You'll do best by filling your minds and meditating on...the best, not the worst; the beautiful, not the ugly; things to praise, not things to curse" (Philippians 4:8, *The Message*). That's how Paul learned to be content, whatever his circumstances, "whether well fed or hungry, whether living in plenty or in want" (Philippians 4:12).

A Larger World

The first step toward a life of awe is learning to look for what is best and most beautiful in each present moment, and that is precisely the purpose of this portion of *Finding God in a Galaxy Far, Far Away*. The coming chapters will equip you to believe in the existence of a larger world, all around you, all the time, and will help you to fill every moment of your life with an intimate awareness of this unseen realm.

So if your present reality has seemed a bit dull lately, prepare yourself for a dramatic change. You're about to experience life in ways that you've never sensed it before! You're about to take, in the words of Obi-Wan Kenobi, your first step into a larger world.

2

"Your Eyes Can Deceive You"

"Your eyes can deceive you. Don't trust them."

OBI-WAN KENOBI
STAR WARS: EPISODE IV—A NEW HOPE

So we fix our eyes not on what is seen, but on what is unseen.
For what is seen is temporary, but what is unseen is eternal.

PAUL
2 CORINTHIANS 4:18

The young apprentice concentrates on the silver sphere that hovers just beyond his reach. The robotic orb quivers slightly, taunting the untrained warrior's lightsaber. The robed Jedi Master seated nearby sees that the boy is reckless, restless, and immature. Yet the boy is learning—learning to sense in his soul what he cannot see with his eyes.

Without warning, the silver sphere lunges at the boy's leg, discharging a brief but stinging bolt of energy. The blast catches the boy in the hip, eliciting a sharp yelp.

The Corellian space pirate in the corner chortles, "Hokey religions and ancient weapons are no match for a good blaster at your side, kid."

"You don't believe in the Force, do you?" the Jedi apprentice asks.

Han Solo's reply is cynical and sharp. "Kid, I've flown from one side of this galaxy to the other. I've seen a lot of strange stuff, but I've never seen anything to make me believe there's one all-powerful force controlling everything. There's no mystical energy field that controls *my* destiny. It's all a lot of simple tricks and nonsense."

A smile plays gently at the corners of the Jedi Master's mouth, as if his aged mind has suddenly recalled some long-forgotten joy. "I suggest you try it again, Luke." Obi-Wan Kenobi places a helmet on the boy's head. The blast shield hides his eyes. "This time, let go of your conscious self and act on instinct."

Luke Skywalker chuckles nervously. "With the blast shield down, I can't even see! How am I supposed to fight?"

"Your eyes can deceive you," Obi-Wan advises. "Don't trust them."

Luke swings wildly at his target. This time, the laser strikes him in the seat of the pants—much to the delight of the space pirate.

"Stretch out with your feelings," the Jedi Master says, soothing his student.

Luke stands still, concentrating. This time, when the sphere dives toward him, he moves deftly to protect himself, thrice deflecting a laser bolt with his lightsaber.

"You see," Obi-Wan encourages the young Jedi. "You *can* do it!"

"You know, I *did* feel something!" Luke's beaming eyes emerge from beneath the helmet. "I *could* almost see the remote!"

"That's good," Obi-Wan replies, relief washing over his face. "You have taken your first step into a larger world."

Looking for a Larger World

A larger world.

Deep inside, isn't that what we all want? A world that's bigger than the bills we can't seem to pay, more satisfying than the chores we can't seem to complete, more promising than the pressures we can't seem to escape?

That's certainly what Luke Skywalker was looking for. Early in *Episode IV—A New Hope,* the farm boy sits in a dingy garage and grumbles to his droid, "I'm never gonna get out of here!... If there's a bright center to the universe, you're on the planet that it's farthest from."

Oh, Lord, you have made us for yourself, and our hearts are restless until they find their rest in you.[1]

AUGUSTINE OF HIPPO

In the next film, we find Luke in the swampy bogs of the planet Dagobah. His uncle's farm is light years away, and Luke is preparing to begin his Jedi training in earnest. Yet restlessness continues to consume him. He complains as he waits for an ancient Jedi Master—the very creature who, unbeknownst to Luke, is already serving him: "I don't want your help. I want my lamp back. I'm gonna need it to get out of this slimy mudhole." Once Luke's training is underway, the discontent strikes again, and he rushes to confront Darth Vader long before he is ready for the burden of knowing that he is the Dark Lord's son.

In light of Luke's spotty record, it isn't surprising that, when Obi-Wan Kenobi urges Yoda to train Luke, the pint-size Jedi Master protests, "This one a long time have I watched. All his life has he looked away...to the future, to the horizon. Never his mind on where he was...what he was doing. Adventure? Heh!

Excitement? Heh! A Jedi craves not these things. You"—the ancient master looks into Luke's anxious eyes—"are reckless!"

Why is this young Jedi so reckless, wildly crisscrossing the solar system in search of adventure? And why does he remain so restless, even after he finds himself embroiled in exploits that surpass his wildest fantasies? The answer should come easily— you and Luke are, after all, on the same quest. Both of you are looking for a larger world.

The Elusive Emptiness

Oh, I know, you've never jumped into an X-wing fighter and plunged across the galaxy, searching for some far-flung adventure to satisfy your restless heart. Yet at some point, you *have* sensed an elusive emptiness deep within your soul. You, too, have felt the desperate longing for something larger, something greater, something *more*.

It's this elusive inner hope that typically triggers the quests that will be told and retold throughout time. Remember the genesis of Frodo's journey in *The Lord of the Rings*?

> Frodo began to feel restless, and the old paths seemed too well-trodden. He looked at maps and wondered what lay beyond their edges… He took to wandering further afield and more often by himself… Often he was seen walking and talking with the strange wayfarers that began at this time to appear in the Shire.[2]

The adventurers' aims may change from one tale to the next, but the restlessness of their hearts remains the same. Frodo Baggins longs to explore the lands that lay beyond the Shire, and

Gollum lusts for the One Ring. Dorothy longs to find a land somewhere over the rainbow, and Perceval wants to touch the Holy Grail. Neo longs to know the truth about the Matrix, and Luke Skywalker is desperate for a larger world than his uncle's moisture farm can provide.

The Reason for Your Restlessness

Your restlessness hasn't sent you careening into Cloud City in search of Darth Vader or creeping into the caverns of Mordor to destroy the One Ring. It probably has, however, sent you to the classifieds in search of a more satisfying career, to the mall in search of a more trendy look, or on a lavish spending spree in a vain attempt to get away from it all. Perhaps it's even sent you to a party or bar where you've discovered that, even if you can't quench your deepest longings, you can at least drown them—for a few hours. Then the morning sun floods anew through your bedroom window, and restlessness rises again to the surface of your soul. Despite your best efforts, you remain like the Israelites, searching for their lost Land of Promise; you carry "a restless heart, longing eyes, a homesick soul" (Deuteronomy 28:65, *The Message*). You still wake up looking for a larger world.

> *We must be fond of this world, even in order to change it… We must be fond of another world…in order to have something to change it to.*[4]
> G. K. CHESTERTON

So what are you supposed to do about these longings? The good news about your restless heart is also the bad news: The reason you long for a larger world is because *you were made for a larger world*. You possess a homesick soul because your true home is a country that your eyes have never seen. You were made for far more than the life you are living right now. You were made for a life of awe.

In the classic *Star Wars* trilogy, even though Luke Skywalker has no clue that his father once stood among the greatest of the Jedi Knights, Luke somehow knows that he is destined for a larger world than his uncle's farm. Likewise, you recognize intuitively that you are destined for far more than this world or your five senses can ever supply. That's what has set your heart on a perpetual quest for *more*. C. S. Lewis summed up your situation in this way:

> Creatures are not born with desires unless satisfaction for these desires exists. A baby feels hunger; well, there is such a thing as food. A duckling wants to swim; well, there is such a thing as water. Men feel sexual desire; well, there is such a thing as sex. [So] if I find in myself a desire which no experience in this world can satisfy, the most probable explanation is that I was made for another world.[3]

At least now you know *why* you long for a larger world—it's because you were made for something more. Yet this raises another unsettling question: If you possess desires that nothing in this world can satisfy, does that mean your soul is destined for perpetual dissatisfaction?

All Around Us, All the Time

The answer depends on how you respond to a single question: *Where is the larger world?* For most people, the answer to this question seems to be "somewhere else." These persons look around them and see nothing that can completely satisfy their restless souls. So they keep looking somewhere else, forever hoping to find fulfillment around the next corner. Seekers of this sort are sprinkled throughout the *Star Wars* saga. Dissatisfied with the scope of his own powers, Anakin Skywalker turns somewhere else—and ends up as Darth Vader, apprentice of the evil Emperor. Unwilling to wait until his Jedi training is completed before he confronts Darth Vader, Luke Skywalker rushes somewhere else—and ends up in a duel that leaves him dangerously close to death at the end of *Episode V—The Empire Strikes Back*.

And you?

Somehow, I suspect that you've spent more time than you care to admit looking "somewhere else." At the end of your quest, perhaps you've ended up with a closet that bulges with clothes you've never worn. Or a waistline that bulges from more calories than you needed (and a soul that's still starving for a larger world). Perhaps you've concluded that the only place you'll ever find a larger world is on the far side of your funeral service. Your "somewhere else" is a heavenly kingdom located at some point in the future.[5] Between here and there, you've resigned yourself to living with a restless heart, longing eyes, and a homesick soul. Your surrender to your own emptiness may be less ominous than Anakin Skywalker's surrender to the dark side of the Force, but it's no less deadly to the health of your soul.

There is hope, though. It's found in another possible reply to the question "Where is the larger world?" Unlike the previous response, this answer doesn't destine your soul for perpetual dissatisfaction. Instead, it sets you on a path toward persistent contentment and pure satisfaction. The reply is this: "All around me, all the time."

I already hear your protest: "But *where*? I don't see it!" And that's precisely the point. *The larger world for which your soul is searching is not a world that your eyes can see.* In every moment of your life, a hidden realm—a vast world of wildness and wonder—surrounds you, gently caressing your innermost self.

The Real World

You've sensed this hidden realm from time to time. Remember when you caught yourself staring into the eastern sky, and it seemed as if, just for a moment, you might be able to reach into the sunrise and stroke the face of God? What about the time you were sitting alone on a distant beach—warm sand and gentle waves kneading your weary feet—and you could sense a divine presence in each breath of sea-saturated air? Or maybe you were standing in church, singing the chorus of a familiar song, when the words suddenly erupted with new meaning and poured heaven's joy into the parched recesses of your soul.

In the aftermath of such encounters, we typically wrench ourselves away from our daydreaming, chide ourselves for

By faith Abraham, when called to go to a place he would later receive as his inheritance, obeyed and went, even though he did not know where he was going... All these people were still living by faith when they died. They did not receive the things promised; they only saw them and welcomed them from a distance... They were longing for a better country.
HEBREWS 11:8, 13, 16

our moment of childlike wonder, and return to the dreary habits that we call "real life."

What we miss is the fact that this unseen realm—the larger world that bursts without warning into the dim routines of our day-to-day lives—is not a far-fetched fantasy, fit for nothing more than silly daydreams. Though this realm can never be captured between the slides of a microscope or pinpointed on any astronomical chart, it *is* the real world. And life in this realm *is* real life. Best of all, it's a reality that's available *here* and *now*. It is woven throughout our everyday lives. Although human eyes rarely glimpse this realm, it is closer to us than the air we breathe, steeping all of life with wonder and filling the visible world with all that is good and lovely and true.

T. S. Eliot once wrote:

> To believe in the supernatural is not simply to believe that after living a successful, material, and fairly virtuous life here one will continue to exist in the best-possible substitute for this world, or that after living a starved and stunted life here one will be compensated with all the good things one has gone without: it is to believe that the supernatural is the greatest reality here and now.[6]

Believing in a Larger World

I desperately want to believe that this unseen world actually surrounds me here and now—and so do you. That's part of the appeal of the *Star Wars* films: They present us with a class of creatures, the Jedi Knights, who actually believe in a world that's larger than terrestrial eyes can see. That's why Obi-Wan Kenobi reminds Luke Skywalker, "Your eyes can deceive you. Don't trust them."

The problem is, I—much like Luke—want to trust my eyes. Yet if I intend to experience a larger world, my eyes are precisely the part of my anatomy that I cannot afford to trust. When I trust my eyes, I become like the religious leaders that Jesus described: "Though seeing, they do not see" (Matthew 13:13). When, however, I begin to believe that the world that matters most is precisely the world that I do not typically notice, an entirely new awareness emerges in my life—one that enables me to begin to live every moment in authentic awe.

Heaven is not a state of mind. Heaven is reality itself. All that is fully real is Heavenly.[7]

C. S. LEWIS

That momentary flash on the horizon that just caught my attention? My eyes tell me to ascribe it to a stray meteor, aging retinas, or perhaps a peculiar reflection on my windshield. Yet what if, just for a moment, the three dimensions in which I subsist couldn't contain the glory of God? What if that fleeting glimmer was an ephemeral glimpse into a larger world? What if, in that instant, the point of demarcation between the visible world and eternity suddenly shifted?

And the drifter on the corner, carrying the battered sign? My eyes tell me to see him as a homeless tramp, a leech upon the flesh of society. Yet we live in a world where saints, prophets, angels—even God Himself—have shown up in the least likely of packages. What if Gabriel and Michael are hanging out in my neighborhood, clutching cardboard signs to hide their angelic splendor? What if Elizabeth Barrett Browning was right when she wrote, "Earth's crammed with heaven, and every common bush afire with God"?[8]

This sort of perspective seems absurd to me too—until I remember how the biblical characters Simeon and Anna saw the salvation of Israel in a baby boy who looked suspiciously like every other little screecher in the Temple nursery (see Luke 2:25–33). Once God has shown up in the flesh of a newborn baby, "those who believe in God can never in a way be sure of him again":

> If holiness and the awful majesty of God were present in this least auspicious of all events, the birth of a peasant's child, then there is no place or time so lowly and earthbound but that holiness can be present there too.[9]

Once He set out on His earthly ministry, the incarnate God never stopped seeing extraordinary possibilities in less-than-ordinary events. He foresaw the future of His kingdom in a dozen dodgy disciples—some of whom weren't particularly good at casting out demons and one of whom wasn't even a believer in the first place (see Matthew 16:19; Mark 9:14–32; Acts 1:16–25). And, most absurd of all, in the midst of my many failings, God manages to notice a glimmer of His glory in even *me* (see 2 Corinthians 4:6–18).

It is a strange thing that many truly spiritual men...have actually spent some hours in speculating upon the precise location of the Garden of Eden. Most probably we are in Eden still. It is only our eyes that have changed.[10]

G. K. CHESTERTON

In a world where God can see something glorious in the ordinary lives of you and me, the possibility of finding divine glory in a gleam on the horizon or in a vagabond on the corner should become infinitely more believable.

The apostle Paul put it like this:

Our lives filled up with light as we saw and understood God in the face of Christ, all bright and beautiful. If you only look at us, you might well miss the brightness... [But] there's far more here than meets the eye. The things we see now are here today, gone tomorrow. But the things we can't see now will last forever. (2 Corinthians 4:6–7, 18, *The Message*)

And here's the best part: I don't have to run to a galaxy far, far away to find this larger world. When I open my life to the glory of God, this larger world already surrounds me, filling my ordinary life with indescribable wonder.

Learn to Live in Awe...

...by believing in a larger world
than your eyes can see.

SPIRITUAL EXERCISES FOR THE SERIOUS PADAWAN

Be Mindful of the True Force

When you find yourself longing for a larger world, what people, places, or diversions do you run to? Daydreams of a different future? The shopping mall? The movies? On a piece of paper, list these people, places, and things. Look carefully at your list. Recognize that even though the items on your list may not be *wrong,* none of them can satisfy the deepest longings of your soul.

Beneath your list, copy 2 Corinthians 4:18. Place a mark through each item on your list. As you cross off each item, choose to "fix your eyes…on what is unseen" throughout the coming week. Set aside specific times this week to meditate on 2 Corinthians 4:18 and to learn to look for the "larger world" around you.

Meditate on the True Force

I am watching the figure two tables away from me
        not with disgust, not with desire—
        simply recognizing his common humanity
        with me and, through the Incarnation,
        with God.
He is reading the paper
        alone,
        the tips of his mouth turned
        toward the world's latest calamity.
Suddenly he looks upward.
Expecting someone?
No, his gaze ranges too far upward
        for any terrestrial being.
His upturned eyes are the silent echo
        of Bethlehem shepherds on the graveyard shift,
        of the souls in Dante's dream,
        of faces strung across the Sistine ceiling,
        of the lost child seeking her father's face.
All of them, though they may know it not,
        silently searching
        for the unseen reflection
        of a larger world.
We are looking,
        all of us,
        for the face of God.

"That Is Why You Fail"

Luke Skywalker: *"I don't... I don't believe it."*
Yoda: *"That is why you fail."*
<small>STAR WARS: EPISODE V—THE EMPIRE STRIKES BACK</small>

"Everything is possible for him who believes."
<small>JESUS
MARK 9:23</small>

Use the Force, yes," Yoda whispers to his apprentice. In the center of the swamp, Luke Skywalker stands on one hand, legs stretched toward a desolate sky. Master Yoda rests serenely on one of the young Jedi's boots. Both creatures appear to be suspended by forces unseen, enfolded in powers unknown. A dingy mist clings to the earth like a vast, soiled blanket.

The pint-size Jedi Master murmurs again, "Now...the stone. Feel it."

A nearby stone drifts into the air. And then, without warning, a tubby blue-and-white droid erupts in a series of frantic chirps and whistles. Luke's focus on the larger world rapidly dissipates.

Sensing Luke's failure to focus, Yoda cries out, "Concentrate!"

But it is too late. Master, apprentice, and stone all crash to the ground.

Frustrated, Luke glowers at his anxious droid, until he notices the source of R2–D2's concern. Luke's starfighter—his only means of escape from this swampy sphere suspended somewhere in the galaxy's outer rim—has slipped into the bog until only its nose remains visible.

"Oh, no," Luke groans. "We'll never get it out now."

"So certain are you." Displeasure saturates Yoda's response. "Always with you it cannot be done. Hear you nothing that I say?"

"Master, moving stones around is one thing. This is totally different."

"No! No different!" Yoda stamps his foot in frustration. "Only different in your mind. You must unlearn what you have learned."

Luke inhales deeply. "All right. I'll give it a try."

"No! Try not," Yoda retorts. "Do. Or do not. There is no try."

Luke concentrates, stretching his fingertips toward the submerged ship. The starfighter shivers slightly, its nose pressing through the trembling surface. Yoda stares in wide-eyed wonder. Then the ship slips from Luke's grasp and sinks deeper into the shadowy bog. Yoda's expression turns downcast. His apprentice has failed again.

"I can't," Luke pants. "It's too big."

"Size matters not," Yoda observes. "Look at me. Judge me by my size, do you?"

Luke shakes his head.

"And well you should not. For my ally is the Force. And a powerful ally it is. Life creates it, makes it grow. Its energy surrounds us and binds us." Yoda's eyes range upward, as if he is drawing his words from a realm that Luke cannot yet see. "You must feel the Force around you."

Luke Skywalker is not convinced. "You want the impossible," he mutters. Turning his back toward Yoda, the student stumbles into the dreary mist. He drops to the ground at the edge of the tangled undergrowth.

The ancient master's brow furrows as he reaches outward toward Luke's ship. Slowly, effortlessly, majestically, the starfighter emerges from the murky waters. R2–D2 whistles and whirs, but Yoda's concentration never wavers.

When Luke Skywalker turns around, he sees his starfighter settling gently on solid ground. Luke gazes in unadulterated awe as he approaches the machine, gingerly grasping the wings as if he is uncertain whether he has witnessed a miracle or wandered into a dream. Finally he looks at his master.

> *"Size matters not."*
>
> YODA, JEDI MASTER
> STAR WARS: EPISODE V—THE
> EMPIRE STRIKES BACK

"I don't... I don't believe it," the young apprentice stammers.

"That"—Yoda's voice is firm, and his eyes quarry the depths of Luke's soul—"is why you fail."

The Road That Leads to the Larger World

"It is one thing to see the land of peace from a wooded mountaintop," St. Augustine once remarked, "but it is quite another to remain on the road that leads there."[1] I think that's what Luke Skywalker discovers during this phase of his Jedi training.

The young Jedi has heard the echoes of a larger world—"the land of peace," in St. Augustine's parlance—in the voice of his departed mentor, Obi-Wan Kenobi. These inner rumblings remained with him when Luke destroyed the first Death Star, when he first learned to wield a lightsaber, and when he managed his escape from an icy cave on the planet Hoth. Now Luke has followed the echoes of a larger world as far as Dagobah, where he has encountered the Jedi Master Yoda.

Yet when the time comes for him to tread the path that will lead him to live in the power of a larger world, Luke mutters to Yoda, "You want the impossible," and turns away. Still mired in the visible world, Luke sees only a massive starfighter steadfastly stuck in the swamp. Unfazed, Yoda reminds Luke of the unseen strength that already surrounds him—"You must feel the Force around you"—and proceeds to set the ship on solid ground.

Why does Luke fail this test? According to Yoda, it's because he does not believe. At first, Yoda's suggestion seems strange. After all, Luke does believe in the *existence* of the Force. He's even aware that the Force can enable him to accomplish a handful of remarkable feats—soaring leaps and long-lasting handstands, the levitation of lightsabers and the lifting of stones.

For the Jedi, however, to believe in the Force is not merely to admit the existence of the Force. It is not even to reach out to the larger world to perform a trifling trick or two. In the *Star Wars* saga, Jedi Knights must believe so deeply in the larger world that they learn to live constantly in its power. Their beliefs must move beyond *mere acknowledgment* and give birth to *faithful commitment*. That's the basis of Yoda's words to Luke Skywalker: "A Jedi must have the deepest commitment, the most serious mind."

This faith-commitment requires the burgeoning Jedi to live according to the Jedi Code and to follow in the footsteps of the masters. Simply put, for the Jedi, faith is not only a way of *thinking about* the larger world but also a way of *living in* the larger world.

Living in the Power of a Larger World

Despite the differences between believing in an impersonal Force and a personal God, this understanding of faith is strikingly similar to the view of faith presented in the Scriptures. Believing in Jesus of Nazareth requires far more than thinking about God in a certain way (see James 2:14–26). "The Word of God is not received by faith when it flits about on top of the brain," John Calvin once commented, "but when it roots itself in the depths of the heart."[2]

Faith, as presented in the New Testament, includes two inseparable aspects. One aspect is subjective—it involves personal commitment to the person of Jesus. This commitment leads to obedience, perseverance, and love (see John 3:36; Romans 5:1–5; 1 Corinthians 13:2; 1 John 3:10). The other aspect is objective confidence—it entails trusting in the conditions, promises, and events through which God has revealed His power (see Romans 10:9; Hebrews 11:3, 6; 1 John 5:1). Together, these two aspects of faith allow the believer to live in a larger world than his or her eyes can ever see (see Hebrews 11:8–16).[3]

Here's how Paul described this sort of life:

> Don't shuffle along, eyes to the ground, absorbed with the things right in front of you. Look up, and be alert to what is going on around Christ—that's where the action is. See things from his perspective... Your real life— even though invisible to spectators—is with Christ in God. He *is* your life. (Colossians 3:2–3, *The Message*)

In the biblical sense of the term, *belief* means not only accepting the existence of a larger world—the world that's "invisible to spectators"—but also *learning to live in the power of this larger world.*

Luke Skywalker had sensed the inner tremors of this invisible world; he had perceived "the land of peace from a wooded mountaintop." Yet when it came to believing so deeply in the larger world that he lived constantly in its power, Luke failed miserably.

So do most of us.

We have glimpsed transient glisterings of the land of peace: the gurgling cry of a newborn baby; the watery wonder of baptism; the echo of the ancient words "This is my body, broken for you"—all standing as fleeting reminders of a larger reality. Yet when it comes to immersing ourselves so deeply in the land of peace that this larger world becomes our native land, its air our native breath, we don't fare nearly as well.

> *"Training to be a Jedi will not be easy. It will be a challenge. And if you succeed, it will be a hard life."*
>
> QUI-GON JINN, JEDI MASTER
> STAR WARS: EPISODE I—
> THE PHANTOM MENACE

For example, in the moments when my uncertainties about future possibilities eclipse the pleasure of my present realities, I could call on the closeness of a larger world and find calmness for my soul. Instead, I allow myself to wallow in the bogs of anger, frustration, and fear. Before it's over, I'm left with a stomach that's upset, muscles that are uptight, and dreams that are upturned, scattered amid the muck and mud of my own anxieties. My awareness of the land of peace shifts from an intimate sense of divine bliss to a vague, unreachable itch in the inner chambers of my soul.

I don't think I'm alone in my dilemma. Most of Christ's followers accept the existence of a larger world, all around us, all the time. Yet we fail so frequently to live in the power of this world that we find ourselves wondering, "Is it possible, in my day-to-day existence, to trust so deeply in a larger world that I become aware of its presence all the time? Can I actually learn to live in the power of a world that I cannot see?"

Who Can Live in the Power of the Larger World?

In the *Star Wars* universe, a deep awareness of the larger world is reserved for creatures whose genetic codes have predisposed them to be sensitive to "the Force." That's why, in *Episode I—The Phantom Menace,* Anakin Skywalker seems to "see things before they happen." For such creatures, training with a Jedi Master opens up even greater possibilities. Anakin manages death-defying leaps. Yoda levitates mammoth objects. And Obi-Wan Kenobi can change a stormtrooper's thoughts with a mere wave of his hand.

After witnessing this intimate interplay between the visible and the invisible realms in the earliest *Star Wars* film, my childhood response was to wonder, "Wow! What if *I* could live in a world like *that*?" Months after watching *Episode IV—A New Hope* for the first time, I still dreamed about being able to change someone's intentions with a wave of my hand. I even tried to perform a few Jedi mind-tricks on my older brother and on the neighbor's cat. The results were not encouraging: My brother walloped me on the head with his fist, and the cat glared at me for a few seconds before yawning and walking away. I concluded at an early age that I was not destined to live in the power of a larger world.

I have since arrived at a more optimistic perspective—one that derives more from Jesus, Paul, and the Hebrew prophets than from the Jedi Council. I've tried to summarize this perspective in a single sentence: *I can live in the power of a larger world by learning to live "as if."* Even when I neither see nor feel any evidence of a larger world, I am called to live *as if* a larger world constantly surrounds me.

Just like Sarah and Abraham, who kept living *as if* their gnarled hands would one day grasp a newborn baby, despite the desolate crib that still haunted their home (see Hebrews 11:8–12).

Just like Moses, who kept living *as if* God was with him, because he once caught a fleeting glimpse of the glory of "him who is invisible" in the shadow of a burning bush (see Hebrews 11:27).

Just like the first disciples, who lived *as if* Jesus still stood among them, even after their Master vanished through a blazing gash in the eastern sky (see Luke 24:50–53; Acts 1:6–14).

How did they do it? These people learned to live *as if* their true home was a larger world than their eyes could ever see. They saw that they were made for far

When do I then have faith? If I do not just believe that what God says is true, but rather put my trust in him, give myself to him, and dare to act with him, and believe without any doubt that he will be with me…

Such a faith which takes that risk in God…be it in life or death, that faith alone makes a true Christian.[4]

MARTIN LUTHER

51

more than the life they were living. They knew they were made for a life of awe.

This perspective is present not only in the pages of Scripture but also in the finest of the fairy tales and epic stories. Despite her stepsisters' cruelty, Cinderella continues to live *as if* she is high-bred and noble-born—and, with the help of a telltale slipper, finally finds herself recognized as the princess that she has always been. Despite shrouding himself in the dark robes of a Ranger, Aragorn continues to carry himself *as if* he is a king—and, in the end, rises to his royal destiny. Despite his diminutive appearance, Jedi Master Yoda lives *as if* "size matters not"—and performs otherwise impossible tasks.

To live *as if* is to recognize that the real hero's quest "lies not in seeking new lands but in seeing with new eyes"[5]—in seeing our lives through the eyes of faith.

Learning to Live "as If"

What does it mean, though, to learn to live "as if" on a practical day-to-day level? I cannot offer you a surefire plan, guaranteed to transport you into a larger world. I *can* tell you that learning to live "as if" doesn't happen instantly. Like the training of a Jedi Knight, learning to live "as if" is a process that I must practice, a difficult path wherein my perspectives and perceptions slowly expand to embrace previously unimagined possibilities.

Learning to live "as if" means that, even when I cannot sense God's closeness, I can choose to live *as if* every atom of oxygen that I draw into my body is aflame with divine glory, for it is in Him that "we live and move and have our being" (Acts 17:28).

Even when I feel like God has forsaken me, I can choose to

live *as if* the whistling of the wind in the hills around me may be the laughter of a vast multitude of angels—a shimmering host that I would see clearly if only I could look at these thousand hills through the eyes of God (see 2 Kings 6:12–17).

Even when it seems like I'm utterly alone, I can choose to live *as if* the saints of the past—Polycarp of Smyrna and Paul of Tarsus, Martin Luther with his theses and Miriam with her tambourine—swirl and twirl through my neighborhood in unseen billows of fire, for Scripture tells me that I am surrounded by "such a great cloud of witnesses" (Hebrews 12:1).

And despite the fact that my actions often suggest otherwise, I can choose to live *as if* my soul is already seated in heaven itself. Isn't this, after all, what the apostle Paul promised? According to Paul, God has already "raised us up with Christ and seated us with him in the heavenly realms" (Ephesians 2:6).

A crazy way to look at life? Perhaps. But then again, lunacy was what Jesus' family ascribed to Him, too. "His family...went to take charge of him, for they said, 'He is out of his mind'" (Mark 3:21). Why did kith and kin look at the boy from Galilee like He was a few bagels short of a baker's dozen? I think it was because he lived every moment of His life as if a larger world surrounded him.

Once without warning, Jesus laughed, looked into the

By an act of faith, Abraham said yes to God's call to travel to an unknown place... Abraham did it by keeping his eye on an unseen city with real, eternal foundations—the City designed and built by God.

HEBREWS 11:8, 10,
THE MESSAGE

The fairy-tale journey may look like an outward trek across plains and mountains, through castles and forests, but the actual movement is inward, into the lands of the soul.[7]

TERRI WINDLING

heavens, and thanked an invisible friend—His heavenly Father—for revealing the larger world to the least likely of people (see Matthew 11:25). Another time, when others heard only a distant thunder, Jesus heard the very voice of God (see John 12:27–30). When everyone else saw six dozen disciples stumbling back to their Master after a successful preaching tour, what Jesus saw was Satan, falling "like lightning from heaven" (Luke 10:18).[6] Jesus lived as if the larger world—the "kingdom of God," in first-century phraseology—grew within Him and around Him in every moment (Luke 17:20–21). And indeed it did.

Stop Looking, Start Living

As far as I know, experiencing a larger world by learning to live "as if" will never enable you to levitate a starfighter or even to stand on one hand for more than a few seconds. The feats that you will perform are, in fact, far greater than anything the Jedi Knights ever imagined: You'll find satisfaction where you previously felt frustration. You'll find the presence of God in the places where you previously felt alone. You may even be able to sense the workings of God where others see only disaster. Such powers may not improve your lightsaber skills, but they will do wonders for your soul.

Best of all, these experiences of a larger world are not intended for a few fortunate creatures who happen to have Force-sensitive cells cavorting through their capillaries. They are available to anyone who's willing to stop looking for a larger world somewhere else and to start living as if the larger world is present here and now. They're for anyone who's willing, in biblical terms, to walk "by faith, not by sight" (2 Corinthians 5:7).

To begin to live as if this larger world is the greatest reality here and now, among us, is to take our first tentative steps into a realm that is far greater than any teller of fairy tales has yet fathomed. And yet, for those who have embraced the One in whom the timeless tales come true, this awe-inspiring kingdom remains as close as our own souls.

Learn to Live in Awe...

...by learning to live "as if."

SPIRITUAL EXERCISES FOR THE SERIOUS PADAWAN

Be Mindful of the True Force

When do *you* fail to live in the power of a larger world? On a piece of paper, list three recent situations in which you did not live as if a larger world was available to you. Beside each item, write these words: "Next time, I will live *as if*…" Finish each sentence with a specific, new perspective that will help you to live this life "as if." For example, if you became angry earlier this week because someone squandered your time, you might write these words beside your description of the situation: "Next time, I will live *as if* God always provides me with enough time to do everything He wants me to do."

Each day this week, make time to review your list. Meditate on Scripture passages that draw your attention to the larger world around you. Mark 1:9–15, Hebrews 11:1–16, and Hebrews 12:1–2 might be appropriate places to start. At the end of the week, spend some time in quiet contemplation simply developing your awareness of the larger world that exists all around you, all the time.

Meditate on the True Force

Once upon a time, I saw the land of peace
    from a mountaintop of my own making.
And it appeared to me that what I needed
to sustain me on this path was
    one more project,
    one more possession,
    one more accomplishment.
But these were detours that sent me
    deep into the land of discontent.
More projects led to too much stress.
More possessions turned into too much stuff.
More accomplishments turned into too much of me.
Then I heard that simple voice,
    still echoing in the distance:
"Follow Me."
"Rest in my footprints."
"Meander in my footsteps."
"Keep me in sight as you walk the path
    to the land of peace."
Swept up in the warm echo of that voice, I realized this:
One day, when I have learned to live as if
You are always with me,
I will move beyond
    all of my stress,
    all of my stuff,
    all of myself.
And I will taste this truth:
Each moment that I spent in Your shadow,
    I was living in the land of peace already.

PART
TWO

"COME WITH ME"

Finding Awe in Fellowship with Others

THE SHIMMERING image of a white-robed princess flickers and fades. The aged Jedi Knight sits in silence, weighing the words he has heard. "This is our most desperate hour," the young senator had said. "Help me, Obi-Wan Kenobi, you're my only hope."

But Obi-Wan Kenobi is not her only hope. No, at this moment, the hope of the galaxy sits at a table in Obi-Wan's hovel, worrying about getting home on time.

A few hours earlier, the boy thought he was searching for a lost droid; in truth, he was looking for a larger world. And, now, Obi-Wan must convince this boy—this restless young man who believes he's nothing more than an orphaned farm boy trapped on a desolate rock in the galaxy's outer rim—that he is made for more than his eyes can see.

Finally, Obi-Wan turns to Luke.

"You must learn the ways of the Force if you're to come with me… I need your help."

And thus Luke Skywalker's journey into the larger world begins.

"If You're to Come with Me…"

When Luke Skywalker sets out on his quest for a larger world, he doesn't do it alone. To complete his quest, the boy needs more than his own meager awareness of the larger world. He needs the wisdom of Obi-Wan Kenobi, the piloting skills of Han Solo, the loyalty of Chewbacca, and the faithful companionship of two cantankerous robots. "Come with me," Obi-Wan says, because he knows that neither he nor Luke can complete the hero's quest alone.

Neither can you.

Despite any delusions you may have to the contrary, you

cannot complete your quest for the larger world on your own.

That's why, in so many timeless myths and fairy tales, a fellowship of improbable sidekicks surrounds the hero. What would *The Chronicles of Narnia* be like if Lucy had tried to rule Narnia alone? It took Lucy and Peter and Susan and even Edmund the deserter to defeat the White Witch and fill the four thrones of Cair Paravel. And what if Dorothy had been the only traveler on the yellow brick road in *The Wonderful Wizard of Oz*? She couldn't have gotten far. And what of *The Lord of the Rings*? Frodo would never have made it to Mordor without Samwise and Merry and Pippin and the Fellowship of the Ring. In every case, the tale's awe-inspiring conclusion becomes possible only because an unlikely band of fellow travelers chose to share the hero's quest. What's more, as they shared this quest, the fellow travelers learned to stand in awe of one another.

> *By yourself you're unprotected. With a friend you can face the worst. Can you round up a third? A three-stranded rope isn't easily snapped.*
> ECCLESIASTES 4:12, *THE MESSAGE*

FRODO: You've left out one of the chief characters: Samwise the stouthearted... Frodo wouldn't have got far without Sam.
SAM: Now, Mr. Frodo, you shouldn't make fun. I was serious.
FRODO: So was I.[1]

Finding Your Fellow Travelers

The purpose of the section that follows is to help you to overcome by pointing out the unlikely band of fellow travelers that

God is using to lead you into a life of awe. But be prepared: Your fellow travelers may not be the persons you expected— they may not even be people that you would *want* to join your journey! In these chapters you will learn to stand in awe of your fellow travelers in the not-quite-perfect community commonly known as the church. You will even learn to look for the presence of Jesus in people who have wronged and hurt you.

Does that sound tough?

It is.

But, hey, if you're willing to believe that a walking carpet called a Wookiee, a Corellian space pirate, and a Jedi long past his prime can partner with a farm boy to save the galaxy, you should be ready for *anything.*

"Our Meeting Was Not a Coincidence"

"Our meeting was not a coincidence.
Nothing happens by accident."

QUI-GON JINN
STAR WARS: EPISODE I—THE PHANTOM MENACE

We were all baptized by one Spirit into one body… There are
many parts, but one body. The eye cannot say to the hand,
"I don't need you!" And the head cannot say to the feet,
"I don't need you!"

1 CORINTHIANS 12:13, 20–21

Two shadows, dark silhouettes etched into a crowded skyline, stand before a vast curved window. Endless rows of repulsor-lifted transports hurtle across the cityscape in crisscross lines so tight that, from a distance, it is difficult to tell where one transport ends and another begins. This is Coruscant, center of the ancient Republic and home of the Galactic Senate for more than a millennium.

The younger man's eyes carefully trace every contour of his lavish surroundings. The massive desk…the peculiar statues…carpets the color of freshly shed blood. Every item in Supreme Chancellor Palpatine's office projects power of a sort untapped among the Jedi Knights—which is, perhaps, why Anakin

Skywalker so deeply relishes his visits to this sumptuous suite. In this place he feels secure, unthreatened—but most of all he feels *powerful*.

"And so, my young Padawan, they have finally given you an assignment." A grandfatherly twinkle glimmers in the pupils of Palpatine's eyes. "Your patience has paid off."

A guilty grin creeps across Anakin's face. The Padawan knows that his patience had nothing to do with the Jedi Council's decision to appoint him as Padmé Amidala's personal protector. If his capacity for patience had played any part in the decision, the council would never have given him the mission. Anakin is impatient, and he knows it.

"Your guidance more than my patience," Anakin admits.

The chancellor's arm slips around Anakin's shoulders. His touch is cordial, almost tender. Almost like the long-lost embrace that every fiber of Anakin's being still craves—the embrace of his mother.

"You don't need guidance, Anakin. In time you will learn to trust your feelings. Then you will be invincible." Every word from the politician's mouth seeps with silky sweetness. "I have said it many times," Palpatine continues, "you are the most gifted Jedi I have ever met."

Anakin Skywalker struggles to hide his euphoria. Ever since his first moments in the Jedi Order, he has been told that he needs the wisdom of the Jedi Masters, he needs the leadership of Obi-Wan, he needs to learn patience and peace. Now, the ruler of the Galactic Republic has confirmed what Anakin has long suspected—that he doesn't need guidance, that he needs only to pursue the power his heart so deeply covets.

Finally, Anakin stammers what he hopes is an appropriate response.

"Thank you, Your Excellency."

Supreme Chancellor Palpatine looks deeply into the young Jedi's brooding eyes.

"I see you becoming the greatest of all the Jedi, Anakin." The chancellor's lips still smile, but his tone has turned solemn, almost foreboding: "Even more powerful than Master Yoda."

When Anakin Skywalker leaves the chancellor's office, the boy is buoyant, sailing on the wild currents of his own pride. As Palpatine watches the Padawan's shadow vanish around the corner, a sinister grin clouds his face. The chancellor has planted a seed in the boy's soul.

A seed of darkness.

In time, the seed will blossom and erupt in a fearsome bloom of black rage and blood-red fire.

Palpatine has planted the seed that will become Darth Vader.

Sith *n., adj.* In the *Star Wars* mythology, the Dark Lords of the Sith are an ancient order that uses the Force for personal power rather than knowledge and defense. Only two Sith Lords exist at any time, a master and an apprentice. The apprentice becomes a master only by murdering his master, then choosing an apprentice of his own.

Do You Really Need Guidance?

"You don't need guidance," the Dark Lord of the Sith says to Anakin. In other words, "You don't need the wisdom of the Jedi Masters. You don't need the fellowship of the Jedi Knights. You can achieve what you want on your own." And from a certain point of view, Anakin *does* achieve what he wants.

What Anakin wants is greater power than any other Jedi. "I am one of the most powerful Jedi," he confesses to Padmé in *Episode III—Revenge of the Sith*, "but I'm not satisfied... I want more." Impatient with the scope of his present powers, Anakin begins to draw his strength from the dark side of the Force. In the process, he becomes so powerful that he is able to destroy hundreds of Jedi single-handedly. He wipes out the leaders of the Trade Federation. His new identity incites gasps of terror throughout the galaxy. And he does it all without his fellow Jedi, simply by giving himself over to his own inner darkness.

But at what cost?

He loses the master who trained him, the woman who loved him, the community that nurtured him. In the end, Anakin is reduced to a scarred scrap of humanity, a fragment of his former self, forever entombed in a suit of lightless armor.

> *"I've become more powerful than any Jedi has ever dreamed of."*
>
> ANAKIN SKYWALKER, JEDI KNIGHT
> *STAR WARS: EPISODE III— REVENGE OF THE SITH*

"You don't need guidance," the Sith Lord says to Anakin. And in one sense, he's right: You *don't* need guidance if your primary longing in life is to gain possessions or power. But if you desire something greater—something such as love, perhaps, or compassion or grace—the guidance of others is something that you simply cannot live without.

You Were Created for Community

Not long after He placed Adam in the Garden of Eden, the Creator of the universe pronounced, "It is not good for the man to be alone" (Genesis 2:18). Why wasn't it good for the man to be alone? Because God had fashioned the man in His own image, and God is never alone.

At the essence of His being, God is an infinite fellowship of Father, Son, and Spirit. Long before God spoke humanity into existence, God the Father and God the Son danced with the Spirit, played dodgeball with the planets, and simply, eternally enjoyed the glorious experience of being *God* (see John 17:1–3). "Let *us* make man in *our* image," God said, in this way signifying that to be formed in God's image is to be created for community (Genesis 1:26, emphasis added). From the very core of our beings, we are creatures formed for intimate communion.

Perhaps that's why the serene fellowship of the ancient Jedi Order appeals so deeply to fans of the *Star Wars* trilogies—it is a distant echo of the communion for which humanity was formed. To become a Jedi is to be committed to a community. Compassion and love are, after all, essential to a Jedi's life, and these qualities can thrive only in the context of committed communion.

Within this community, every Jedi needs guidance and no Jedi stands alone. Every youngling has a teacher, every Padawan has a guide. Not only do the Jedi draw wisdom from living mentors, but they also absorb the teachings of past masters. At the height of the Jedi Order, the Jedi Archives enshrine the ancient masters' insights in millions of holocrons, so that present and future Jedi can share their wisdom. After the fall of the ancient order, the remaining Jedi still draw wisdom from past masters: At the end of *Episode III—Revenge of the Sith,* Yoda informs Obi-Wan that, while in exile on Tatooine, Obi-Wan will continue to learn from his departed Jedi Master, Qui-Gon Jinn. When Luke Skywalker dives into the Death Star's deadly trenches in *Episode*

IV—A New Hope, the voice of his late master, Obi-Wan, urges him to "use the Force." In the closing moments of *Episode VI—Return of the Jedi*, Luke's communion with the specters of Yoda, Obi-Wan, and his father, Anakin, reminds the viewer that, even in death, the Jedi are drawn together. Every part of a Jedi's existence is inherently communal, a matter of doing life together.

Not surprisingly, the fall of the Jedi Order occurs when the Jedi are *not* together. In *Episode III—Revenge of the Sith,* when one of their own joins with millions of clones to destroy the Jedi Order, the Clone Wars have scattered the Jedi throughout the galaxy. The knights are captains and generals of armies, each one far from their fellow Jedi. Separated from one another's strength and wisdom, the Jedi are easily destroyed.

> "You have made a commitment to the Jedi Order, Anakin. A commitment not easily broken."
>
> OBI-WAN KENOBI,
> JEDI MASTER
> STAR WARS: EPISODE II—
> ATTACK OF THE CLONES

The lesson?

It is impossible to remain a Jedi alone.

That's why Palpatine's words to Anakin are so perilous: A Jedi who believes that he needs no guidance opens himself to the dark paths of impatience and pride. "I worry when you speak of jealousy and pride," Obi-Wan tells Anakin before his apprentice's fall to the dark side. "Those are not Jedi thoughts. They're dangerous, dark thoughts." Such thoughts are dangerous and dark because they feed Anakin's arrogant delusion that he does not need the community of Jedi in order to become strong.

The Seed of Darkness

A galaxy far, far away isn't the only place where this insidious seed of self-sufficiency has taken root. This same seed of darkness has been planted in your heart and mine, not by a Dark Lord of the Sith, but by the Master of Lies (see John 8:44). This seed was sown in the human heart by the serpent who whispered into the ear of Eve, "When you eat…you will be like God, knowing good and evil" (Genesis 3:5). Put another way, "Once you eat this fruit, you won't need guidance any longer. You will learn to trust your own feelings. You will become invincible." And thus the human race, like a fictional young Jedi in a faraway galaxy, embraced the delusion that we do not need one another's guidance. Deep inside, each of us wants to determine for ourselves the direction of our lives. One of a toddler's first complete sentences is typically "I can do it myself."

One who seeks solitude without fellowship perishes in the abyss of vanity, self-infatuation, and despair.[4]

DIETRICH BONHOEFFER

Yet following God—like becoming a Jedi Knight—can never be accomplished on one's own. It is pursued in fellowship with others who have embraced the same quest, or it is not pursued at all.

Before the serpent wended his way into the midst of Eden, God created a *community*—he formed not one but two humans and commanded them to rejoice in one another's company (see Genesis 1:27–31; 2:18–25). Later, when the Creator conscripted Abraham for divine service, God's deepest desire was for him to father a fellowship of divine glory (see Genesis 12:1–3). Still later, when God's glory burst through a bush and seized the attention of the shepherd Moses, God's plan was to bind Abraham's offspring together into a faithful community (see Exodus 3:7–10).

So it shouldn't surprise us that, when the incarnate God kicked off His earthly ministry, one of His first tasks was to gather a fellowship of followers. The same serpent who slipped into Eden tried to stop this new creation, of course. He slithered into the deserts of Judea and hissed into the hungering Messiah's ear, "If you are the Son of God, tell this stone to become bread" and "I will give you all their authority and splendor, for it has been given to me, and I can give it to anyone I want to" (Luke 4:3, 6). In other words, "You don't need to use your power for the benefit of others! You don't need to build a community! You don't need to share your glory with your Father! Trust your own feelings." Still, Jesus persisted in His Father's plan and gathered a dozen disciples whose primary task was simply to "be with him" (Mark 3:14).

> There may be religions that come to you through quiet walks in the woods, or by sitting quietly in the library with a book, or rummaging around in the recesses of your psyche. Christianity is not one of them. Christianity is inherently communal, a matter of life in the Body... Jesus did not call isolated individuals to follow Him. He called a group of disciples. He gathered a crowd.[1]

And what did God want out of all this? What was God's purpose in forming a community? He wanted His glorious presence to be so obvious in this ragtag crowd that the entire world would stand in awe (see Isaiah 43:4–7). Wasn't that the point of Jesus' high-priestly prayer? "I have given them the glory that you gave me, that they may be one as we are one…to let the world know that you sent me" (John 17:22–23). That's what it means to be drafted into this adventure that we call the Christian life.

Living in Awe, Living in Fellowship

If I imitate the example of Jesus, I must give up the arrogant delusion that my salvation, my spiritual life, and my sins are personal matters. I must admit that I cannot follow Jesus alone any more than I can get married alone.[2] To follow Jesus, I need the fellowship of others who have chosen to share this quest. So do you, and so has every other follower of Jesus in every time and in every place.

Until I allow God to infuse this truth into my life, I cannot live in awe and my soul remains desperately hungry, restless for a larger world. So what's the solution? Take a look at this description of the earliest believers in the book of Acts:

> Everyone was *filled with awe*, and many wonders and miraculous signs were done by the apostles. All the believers were together and had everything in common… Every day they continued to meet together in the temple courts. They broke bread in their homes and ate together with glad and sincere hearts. (Acts 2:43–44, 46, emphasis added)

The people were "filled with awe"—but at what? Sure, there were some signs being performed, courtesy of the apostles. But most of what these believers were doing was simply *being together*—caring for one another, meeting with one another, eating with one another. The earliest believers shared their lives, and this sharing filled them with awe. The call to live in awe is a call to live in fellowship.

I suggested earlier that *nothing in your life is ordinary*. To take this statement seriously means not only that every *event* in your life is extraordinary but also that every *person* who crosses your path is extraordinary. C. S. Lewis put it this way:

> There are no *ordinary* people. You have never talked to a mere mortal… It is immortals whom we joke with, work with, marry, snub, and exploit… Next to the Blessed Sacrament itself, your neighbor is the holiest object presented to your senses. If he is your Christian neighbor, he is holy in almost the same way, for in him also Christ…is truly hidden.[3]

You were made for far more than a life of petty bickering with your brothers and sisters in Christ. You were made to stand in awe.

Standing in Awe of One Another

When I look at my fellow believers, I frequently *do* stand in awe. As I contemplate the crazy collection of fellow travelers that surrounds me on Sunday mornings, I see a glorious mosaic of grace—young and old, rich and poor, brown and black and white, all drawn to this place by the grace of God. And I stand amazed at these tangible evidences of divine glory around me.

Most of the time.

But there are some folk in my church who I'm fairly certain

I could do without. Like the people whose political preferences don't mesh with mine. Like the people who refuse to help in the preschool department. Like the people who persist in singing off-key during times of praise and worship. Like…well, like all the people who aren't like *me*. Come to think of it, if everyone *could* be just like me, the church would be a much better place.

And now I will show you the most excellent way. If I speak in the tongues of men and of angels, but have not love, I am only a resounding gong or a clanging cymbal… Love is patient, love is kind.

1 CORINTHIANS 12:31–13:1, 4

Or so I believe, in those moments when I give in to the serpent's soft-whispered lie: "You don't need guidance."

But the people whom God has placed in my church *aren't* like me—and that's precisely the point. They aren't supposed to be. Part of the scandal of the cross of Christ is that the persons who rub shoulders in the shadow of His cross are folk that the world would never dream of mingling together (see 1 Corinthians 1:18, 23–26; Galatians 3:28).

So what's God's purpose in placing people together whose practices and preferences are so different? They are divine reminders that church is not about my personal tastes or desires. In fact, it's not about *me* at all. It's about plunging my life into a mismatched community of recovering sinners, bound together by a Spirit whom none of us has ever seen. Because God Himself is present in them, these people are my guides on this journey to the Promised Land, and I need every one of them.

Nothing Happens by Accident

Whenever I embrace the lie that I do not need the guidance of my fellow believers, I—much like Anakin after his fall into the darkness—am reduced to a mere fragment of what I was meant to be.

So are you.

Without your fellow believers, your Christian life will always lack the wildness and wonder that comes from seeing God's presence in the least likely people and places.

You may be asking at this point, "But *how*? How can I possibly see God's presence in these failure-prone folk who make up my community of faith? And *stand in awe* of them? You've got to be kidding!"

Christis is in you, therefore you can look forward to sharing in God's glory.
COLOSSIANS 1:27, THE MESSAGE

I wish that I could supply you with a seven-step plan guaranteed to teach you to stand in awe of your fellow believers. I can't. To be honest, I'm still struggling to finish the first step (which is, I suspect, the only step, but it's a long, *long* step). This first step is encapsulated in Qui-Gon Jinn's comment to Anakin's mother in *Episode I—The Phantom Menace*. "Our meeting was not a coincidence," the Jedi Master says. "Nothing happens by accident." In other words, "Despite the difficulties before us, I believe that it was the plan of a power greater than ourselves that brought us together."

Suppose you looked at your fellow believers in this way— as if no one in your class or congregation is there by accident; as if your meeting was not a coincidence; as if God may have meticulously mingled this particular mixture of people in this particular time and place for a purpose that none of you yet knows. Wasn't that Paul's point in his letter to the Corinthian church?

> All kinds of [gifts] are handed out by the Spirit, and to all kinds of people! The variety is wonderful... All these gifts have a common origin, but are handed out one by one by the one Spirit of God. (1 Corinthians 12:7–8, 11, *The Message*)

"Our meeting was not a coincidence," Qui-Gon says. "Nothing happens by accident." It's true in a galaxy far, far away, and it's true here and now in *your* galaxy. There are no accidental members in the family of faith.

That's why you need the guidance of the fellow believers in your community of faith—none of them is there by accident, and the Spirit of God is working in each of them. They may—like Edmund in Narnia, Boromir in Middle-Earth, and Anakin in a galaxy far, far away—falter and fail. But your fellowship with them is not human coincidence; it is divine providence.

> *"Nothing happens by accident... Finding [Anakin] was the will of the Force."*
>
> QUI-GON JINN, JEDI MASTER
> STAR WARS: EPISODE I—
> THE PHANTOM MENACE

So look at the faces in your fellowship of faith—the ones you love, as well as the ones you'd rather not—and stand in awe. For *here,* in this least likely of places, is the presence of God. And you *do* need their guidance.

Are you ready to stand in awe of your fellow believers?

Great! Not certain where to start?

Well, you know that church member who annoys you? (Yes,

that one.) How about asking her family out to lunch after church on Sunday? (I know, I know, you'd just as soon kiss a Wookiee—but, remember, the Spirit of God is present in her, too.)

Lunch may not bring balance to the Force, but it could do wonders for the fellowship in your church.

Learn to Live in Awe...

...by seeing that there are no accidental members in the family of faith.

SPIRITUAL EXERCISES FOR THE SERIOUS PADAWAN

Be Mindful of the True Force

Prayerfully envision the faces in your community of faith. As you envision each face, make a list of fellow believers with whom it's difficult for you to get along. Now carefully read Ephesians 4:2–6. Beside each name, write one specific way that you can "be patient" and "completely humble and gentle" as you relate to that person. Every day this week, review Ephesians 4:2–6. Pray specifically for God to change your attitude toward each person on your list.

Meditate on the True Force

Lord of all creation,
Lord of all creatures,
Lord of the church,
It's easy to love Your church.
It's not so easy to love certain members of Your church.
You prayed to Your Father,
> *"I want them to be one even as We are one."*

You commanded Your first followers,
> *"Love one another, just as I have loved you."*

Did You really mean it?
> *Are You sure?*
> *No exceptions?*
> *Everyone?*
> *Even…You-know-who?*

Could it be that Your words were a promise and a command?
When you commanded, "Love one another,"
> *were You also promising,*
> *"You will be able to love one another"?*

When You prayed, "I want them to be one,"
> *Were You also promising,*
> *"They will be able to be one"?*

I certainly hope so.
Help me to see that I cannot truly love You
> *unless I also love Your people.*
> *All of them.*
> *Even…You-know-who.*

5

"You Were My Brother"

Anakin: *"I hate you!"*
Obi-Wan: *"You were my brother, Anakin. I loved you!"*
STAR WARS: EPISODE III: REVENGE OF THE SITH

*"Love your enemies. Help and give without expecting a return.
You'll never—I promise—regret it. Live out this God-created
identity the way our Father lives toward us, generously and
graciously, even when we're at our worst."*

JESUS
LUKE 6:35, THE MESSAGE

The Mustafar system will never be a popular vacation spot. It probably won't even be a popular place of escape. Mustafar is a system of last resort.

There is no native life on the twin planets of this system. The rain is bitter acid, the rivers are boiling lava, and the sole continent is a jagged mass of igneous rock, suspended in a sea of smoldering magma. Constant cataclysms—earthquakes and volcanoes of magnitudes unknown on more civilized worlds—are still molding the landscape of this desolate system.

The dual spheres of Mustafar are young, volatile, and dangerous.

Much like a certain young Jedi whose dark mission has landed him here.

78

Trapped inside a makeshift control center on one of the planets, the young Jedi circles a conference table, glowering at the man who was once his master. The man who has been like a father to him. The man who is here to stop his free fall into the darkness.

"Don't make me destroy you, Master," the young Jedi speaks evenly, skillfully masking the fear and fury that wrestle in the depths of his soul. "You're no match for the dark side." His iridescent saber twitches, tracing menacing ellipses of light in the air.[1]

"I've heard that before, Anakin." Obi-Wan Kenobi makes no attempt to hide his wrenching anguish. "But I never thought I'd hear it from you."

Before Obi-Wan can complete his sentence, Anakin Skywalker has lunged across the table, lightsaber thirsty for his master's blood—but Obi-Wan has already sensed his student's sinister intent. The Jedi Master meets Anakin in midair, snatching the younger Jedi's lightsaber even as his own weapon slips from his grasp. Obi-Wan quickly calls on the Force to retrieve his own saber…and, then, for the most infinitesimal segment of time, Obi-Wan Kenobi hesitates.

Hesitates to cleave Anakin's head from his body.

Hesitates to take from Anakin what the young Jedi-turned-Sith has already stolen from a host of unsuspecting innocents. Mace Windu and Shaak Ti. Whie and the other Jedi younglings. All so full of life, now dead.

Hesitates because, despite the depth of Anakin's atrocities, Obi-Wan still loves the boy…still hopes…

The younger man senses his former master's hesitation and seizes the opportunity. Anakin's lightsaber leaps from Obi-Wan's grasp, returning to its dark master's hand.

"The flaw of power is arrogance," Obi-Wan murmurs.

"You hesitate," his fallen student sneers. "The flaw of compassion."

Anakin Skywalker lunges at Obi-Wan again, and their struggle erupts in never-before-seen fury. The room appears to implode as both combatants call on the powers of the Force, hurling objects at one another. A blast door bursts open, and Obi-Wan is forced out of the control room, onto a thin power conduit that traverses the lava sea.

Beneath the two Jedi, the surface of Mustafar ripples and heaves, a vast mantle of molten rock. Crimson and ginger flames lash upward from the inferno like fiery fingers, straining to join the furious melee above. The two warriors tumble downward, eventually finding their footing on platforms that have been caught in a blistering stream of magma.

"This is the end for you, Master," Anakin Skywalker announces as he lifts his lightsaber. "I wish it were otherwise."

Without warning, Obi-Wan hurtles from the precarious platform and lands in the spongy ash at the river's edge.

"It's over, Anakin," Obi-Wan calls. "I have the high ground."

"You underestimate my power!" the younger Jedi bellows in return.

"Don't try it," Obi-Wan whispers—but Anakin already has.

Anakin hurls himself toward Obi-Wan, his sword a blazing sheet of shimmering sapphire. But Obi-Wan Kenobi is ready.

Two strokes.

Two strokes are all that it takes to end the duel.

The first stroke slices through Anakin's knees, searing flesh and bones.

The second stroke severs the young Jedi's wrist. Left hand and lightsaber tumble into the ashes as Anakin crumples beside the lava sea. The mechanical digits of his remaining hand struggle to gain a hold on the blackened bank, but they cannot. His body slips into the lake of fire, and boiling lava begins to creep up his mangled legs.

"You were the Chosen One!" Obi-Wan Kenobi cries, his stomach convulsing as he surveys his brutal handiwork. "It was you who would bring balance to the Force, not leave it in darkness!"

Anakin Skywalker's clothing bursts into flames, and the boy begins to scream. Anguish floods Obi-Wan's soul and spills from his eyes in the form of bitter tears. He cannot bear this torment any longer. He picks up Anakin's lightsaber and begins to walk away.

But he cannot.

Obi-Wan Kenobi turns to take one last look into the eyes of this boy that he has raised, this warrior who has tumbled headlong into the darkness. He longs to see some sign of repentance or remorse—the slightest glimmer of hope.

"Anakin was a good friend... I thought...he could be turned back to the good side. It couldn't be done. He is more machine now than man. Twisted and evil."

OBI-WAN KENOBI,
JEDI MASTER
*STAR WARS: EPISODE VI—
RETURN OF THE JEDI*

Instead, he hears the shrieks of a creature completely twisted by evil.

"I..."

"...hate..."

"...you!"

Anakin Skywalker's final words rip a gash in Obi-Wan's soul deeper than any lightsaber could ever have reached.

Obi-Wan hears another voice speaking in reply and realizes

that it must be his own: "You were my brother, Anakin," he chokes. "I loved you."

Perhaps the most rational act that the Jedi Master could perform at this moment would be to put Anakin out of his misery. But Obi-Wan is still a Jedi, and Jedi Knights do not kill those who are helpless or unarmed—not even those that have fallen as far as Anakin Skywalker.

The Jedi Master releases his fallen brother to the will of the Force.

With this, he turns away. And yet, a part of his heart will always remain on that blackened beach, forever whispering to whatever is left of Anakin Skywalker, "You were my brother. I loved you."

The Longing for Revenge

Have you been to Mustafar lately? Oh, I know you've never set foot on the seething surface of this fictive system. But you *do* know what it's like to be hurt by someone you love, don't you?

You have felt the bitter gall of betrayal swill the last remnants of wonder and awe from your soul.

You know what Obi-Wan felt as he watched his shining star—the young man who had been his closest companion—fade into darkness.

You have stood on the blackened banks of your own broken heart, whispering to someone who has betrayed you, "You were my brother"—or "my husband" or "my mother" or "my father" or "my friend"—"and I loved you."

You *have* been to Mustafar, haven't you?

Whenever you feel betrayed, the first emotion you feel is probably emptiness. If you allow this emptiness to fester and fill with rage, your emptiness becomes the birth canal of a far darker emotion: The dark dragon of revenge rises from the ashes within you, promising to heal your wounds by wounding your offender.

This longing for revenge is almost as ancient as the human race. After all, wasn't it vengeance that fed the rage of Cain as he bludgeoned his brother to death? (See Genesis 4:3–16.) And what about Lamech, the offspring of Cain who murdered a man and proudly pronounced, "If Cain is avenged seven times, then Lamech seventy-seven times" (Genesis 4:24)?

Oh, I know you don't actually plan to *kill* the people who have hurt you. Still, you rejoice when misfortune tumbles into their lives, smirking at the fact that they've finally gotten what they deserved. Perhaps you even deepen your own bitterness by replaying their wrongs in the theater of your mind. And even if you'd never dream of damaging their bodies, you're more than willing to bludgeon their character to death with the club of your words. If so, you have pitched your tent far from the land of awe and deep in a barren desert named Revenge.

The problem with your longing for revenge is that it isn't hurting the person who wounded you nearly as much as it's hurting *you.*

Frederick Buechner put it most picturesquely when he wrote:

> To lick your wounds, to smack your lips over griev-ances long past, to roll over your tongue the prospect of bitter confrontations still to come, to savor to the last toothsome morsel both the pain you are given and the pain you are giving back—in many ways it is a feast fit for a king. The chief drawback is that what you are

wolfing down is yourself. The skeleton at the feast is you.[2]

But maybe you're tired of living in the realm of revenge. Perhaps you're ready to pull up your tent stakes and find a place of inner peace. Perhaps you'd like to feel the refreshing rain of compassion once again—even if it means feeling compassion toward someone who has hurt you. If so, there's a vital lesson for you in the lives of the Jedi Knights.

Releasing the Longing for Revenge

To be a Jedi Knight is to learn to release all fear, anger, and hatred. This release is required because, in the words of Master Yoda, "Fear leads to anger, anger leads to hate, hate leads to suffering." That's also why revenge is forbidden among the Jedi—revenge requires hatred and rage.

It is perhaps at this point that the noble knights of the Jedi Order and the Dark Lords of the Sith differ most radically: Among the Jedi, compassion is central, and every longing for revenge must constantly be released. Among the devotees of the dark side of the Force, rage and revenge are virtues while compassion is a vice.

Remember the words of Darth Maul in *Episode I—The Phantom Menace*? As his dark master unleashes him against the Jedi, the Sith warrior gloats, "At last, we will have revenge." In *Episode II—Attack of the Clones*, Anakin Skywalker takes his first steps toward the dark side when he avenges his mother's death by slaughtering an entire community of Sand People. In *Episode III—Revenge of the Sith*, when Anakin murders a disarmed Count Dooku, the Sith Lord Palpatine brushes aside the dark deed by ascribing it to a normal longing for vengeance: "It is only natural," Palpatine reassures the disillusioned Jedi. "He cut off your arm, and you wanted revenge." Rage and revenge are the fuels that feed the dark powers of the Sith—that is, after all, why their moment of triumph in the third chapter of the *Star Wars* saga is known as the *revenge* of the Sith.

> *Go ahead and be angry. You do well to be angry—but don't use your anger as fuel for revenge. And don't stay angry… Don't give the Devil that kind of foothold in your life.*
>
> EPHESIANS 4:26–27, *THE MESSAGE*

Two decades later, in *Episode VI— Return of the Jedi*, the Sith Lords still view compassion as a weakness and vengeance as a strength: As Darth Vader and Emperor Palpatine make plans to lure Luke Skywalker toward the dark side of the Force, Palpatine murmurs, "Compassion…will be his undoing"—and it almost is.

Still, the Jedi Knights know that without compassion they are no better than the vilest Sith. That's why, even after seeing his student slaughter the Jedi younglings and bow to the despicable Darth Sidious, Obi-Wan Kenobi refuses to resort to revenge. Faced with the prospect of taking the life of an unarmed Sith or releasing him to the powers of a larger world, Obi-Wan chooses the path of compassion and walks away.

Jedi Compassion or Jesus' Compassion

When it comes to compassion and revenge, the mythology of *Star Wars* has much in common with many world religions, including Judaism and Christianity. "Do not seek revenge or bear a grudge against one of your people… It is mine to avenge; I will repay," the Lord commands in the Hebrew Scriptures (Leviticus 19:18; Deuteronomy 32:35). Later Scriptures echo this outlook: "Do not take revenge, my friends," Paul writes to the Roman church, "but leave room for God's wrath" (Romans 12:19)—in other words, be willing to release your longings for revenge to the powers of a larger world. Such a choice does *not* mean that you should act as if others' offenses don't matter. It doesn't even mean that you should never feel upset (see Ephesians 4:26). It simply means that you have released your enemies' punishment to a power greater than yourself. It means that you're refusing to wallow in your rage.

There is also, however, a radical difference between the ethics of the ancient Jedi Knights and the expectations of Jesus Christ. Among the Jedi, it is enough simply to walk away from an enemy, releasing any feelings of hatred and rage; such was the great compassion of Obi-Wan Kenobi on the banks of Mustafar. And if I had to, I suppose that I could follow Obi-Wan's example. If I worked hard enough, I could learn to walk away from the one who has wronged me, releasing my right to demand revenge—and I would feel pretty confident in my capacity for compassion.

After all, what more could God ask for?

A *lot* more, as it turns out.

For those who take their stand in the shadow of the cross, it isn't enough simply to release every inner longing for revenge. Passive release must grow into active love. Remember the words of Jesus? "Love your enemies, do good to those who hate you, bless those who curse you" (Luke 6:27–28). Such is the greatest compassion of all: the compassion of God, expressed in Jesus.

Loving our enemies sounds wonderful, even inspiring—as long as we keep the concept embalmed within the bindings of our Bibles, far from our daily routines. But when we open ourselves to the full implications of this truth, allowing it to penetrate the day-to-day patterns of our lives...well, to put it mildly, the situation becomes much more complicated.

> "Love your enemies. Let them bring out the best in you, not the worst. When someone gives you a hard time, respond with the energies of prayer for that person."
>
> LUKE 6:27–28, *THE MESSAGE*

When I take Jesus' command seriously, nothing in my life can stay the same. It's no longer enough merely to keep my middle finger firmly wrapped around the steering wheel when the cretin in the black SUV cuts me off; I must make a conscious choice to care about his soul. It's no longer enough to ignore the lies that someone is spreading about me; I must find a way to bless the scandal-monger. It's no longer enough to walk away from former friends who now work against me; I must pray that God will prosper their pursuits according to His will (Philippians 1:15–18).

I must be compassionate as God Himself is compassionate, recognizing that my heavenly Father forgives my many failures only to the degree that I forgive the failures of others (see Matthew 5:10–12, 44).

Why? Because you and I were made for far more than a life of bitterness and grudge bearing. We were made for a life of awe.

"I Have a Bad Feeling About This"

When I consider the extreme implications of God's compassion, I suddenly have—to quote the line that makes an appearance in every *Star Wars* film—"a bad feeling about this." I have a bad feeling about whether I have what it takes to live like Jesus lived. I have a bad feeling about my capacity to love people who have wronged me, lied about me, and worked against me. I have a bad feeling about *me*.

So what is it that I'm lacking? If I'm a follower of Jesus, I already possess divine power (2 Timothy 1:7–10). Inasmuch as I allow the Holy Spirit to work in me, I have divine desires (Philippians 2:13). Yet even with divine power and divine desires, I still lack the compassion of Jesus.

Why?

What do I still need?

What I need is a better imagination.

Yes, that's right—imagination.

At its core, faith in Jesus is an exercise of the imagination. The presence of God showing up in the guise of ordinary people; the Spirit of God speaking through the words of saints long gone; the power of God surging into our souls through bread and wine and waters of baptism—every vital experience of the life of faith requires *imagination*. When I fail to stand in awe of God, it's because I have failed to imagine that every earthly event is permeated with His resplendent presence. When I pursue the fleeting pleasure of sin, it's because I have failed to imagine that the presence of God can provide "eternal pleasures" (Psalm 16:11). When I fail to follow Jesus fully, it is not primarily a failure of my faith; it is a failure of the imagination that feeds my faith.

So what does this have to do with loving my enemies?

Everything.

If I claim to follow Jesus, God calls me to imagine the potential of His presence not only in the best and most beautiful—in the wonder of His creation and in the fellowship of my church—but also in the worst.

In people who are down-and-out.

In people who don't behave according to my standards.

Perhaps even in the people I would prefer to despise.

Isn't that the point of Jesus' parable about the final judgment? The King of the universe separates all of His creatures, sending the sheep to His right and the goats to His left. Then He speaks to those on His right:

> "Come, you who are blessed by my Father... I was hungry and you gave me something to eat, I was thirsty and you gave me something to drink, I was a stranger and you invited me in, I needed clothes and you clothed me, I was sick and you looked after me, I was in prison and you came to visit me...
>
> "I tell you the truth, whatever you did for one of the least of these brothers of mine, you did for me."
>
> Then he will say to those on his left, "Depart from me, you who are cursed, into the eternal fire prepared for the devil and his angels. For I was hungry and you gave me nothing to eat, I was thirsty and you gave me nothing to drink, I was a stranger and you did not invite me in, I needed clothes and you did not clothe me, I was sick and in prison and you did not look after me... I tell you the truth, whatever you did not do for one of the least of these, you did not do for me." (Matthew 25:34–35, 40–43, 45)

May I paraphrase Jesus' point? "Whenever you look at someone in need, look beyond what you see and imagine *Me*." This includes people whose deepest needs are forgiveness and love. This even includes your enemies and mine. "God comes to us in the hungry man that we do not have to feed, comes to us in the lonely man we do not have to comfort, comes to us in all the desperate human need of people everywhere that we are always free to turn our backs upon."[3]

> *If you want to change a people's obedience, you must change their imagination.*[4]
> PAUL RICOUER

So when you look at someone who has wronged you, try asking yourself, *What might this person become, if only Jesus lived within him? How might this person change, if only I treated her as someone in whom the very presence of God longs to live? How can I look at this enemy and imagine Jesus?*

You see, the greatest imagination of all isn't the sort that my daughter and I employ when we recreate epic lightsaber duels in our living room. (Well, we *used to* stage our skirmishes in the living room; then we almost broke a lamp and Darth Mommy sent all future battles to the backyard. She's just jealous because *she* doesn't have a lightsaber.) The greatest imaginations aren't even the ones that come up with fairy-tale fantasies in faraway galaxies. The greatest imagination of all is the one that looks at outcasts and enemies and sees something greater in them than they can see in themselves. This imagination doesn't lead to swordfights or space operas but to a simple pathway that winds through the darkest valleys of our lives and emerges in a boundless country known as Compassion.

What an Imagination

Obi-Wan Kenobi may have lacked this sort of imagination as he stood beside the lava sea, but later the son of Anakin Skywalker learned to see something greater in his enemy than his enemy could see in himself. Luke Skywalker learned to *imagine*.

Clothe yourselves with compassion.
COLOSSIANS 3:12

When Luke encounters Darth Vader on the forest moon of Endor, he looks past the sinister armor and sees the troubled young man that Obi-Wan left on the blackened banks of Mustafar. Remember their conversation in *Episode VI—Return of the Jedi*?

LUKE: I've accepted the truth that you were once Anakin Skywalker, my father.

VADER: [turning in anger] That name no longer has any meaning for me!

LUKE: It is the name of your true self. You've only forgotten. I know there is good in you…

VADER: Obi-Wan once thought as you do… It is too late for me, my son.

Despite the Dark Lord's denial, Luke continues to imagine that goodness still remains in Vader's heart. Even when his father allows him to suffer the Emperor's wrath, the son of Skywalker steadfastly refuses to let go of his compassion. And in the end, Luke Skywalker is proven right. His father's final act is to destroy the Emperor, and his final words to his son are these: "You were right about me. Tell your sister…you were right."

In commanding us to forgive, Jesus is inviting us to take charge, to turn the world around, to throw a monkey wrench in the eternal wheel of retribution and vengeance. We don't have to silently suffer the hurt, to lick our wounds, lying in wait for the day when we shall at last be able to return the blow that was dealt to us. We can take charge, turn things around, be victors rather than victims. We can forgive.[7]

WILLIAM WILLIMON AND STANLEY HAUERWAS

Overlooking the lava seas of Mustafar, Anakin Skywalker saw Obi-Wan's hesitation as the flaw of compassion. And on the blackened banks of a broken heart, compassion *can* feel like a weakness. But in the *Star Wars* saga, compassion outlasts revenge, and Luke's imagining that some fragment of goodness remains in Darth Vader finally destroys the darkness.[5]

It's no different in real life.

Remember the life of a certain Jewish carpenter, a long time ago in a land not that far away? He had a habit of always seeing more in others than they could see in themselves. He was betrayed and wounded in ways far worse than the Jedi Knights could ever have imagined. Yet He looked into the eyes of His betrayer and whispered, "Friend" (Matthew 26:50). He stared at the soldiers whose spittle still mingled with the blood and tears in His beard and said, "Father, forgive them" (Luke 23:34). He embraced the disciple who had denied Him and whispered, "Feed my lambs" (John 21:15). And to this day, He looks at the likes of you and me and says, "You are the light of the world" (Matthew 5:14).

What an imagination.[6]

Learn to Live in Awe...

...by imagining the presence of
Jesus in everyone who has a need.

SPIRITUAL EXERCISES FOR THE SERIOUS PADAWAN

Be Mindful of the True Force

List several hurtful experiences from your own life. Beneath your list, copy Leviticus 19:18. Carefully read this text.

During your times of prayer this week, meditate on the words of Jesus in Luke 6:27–36. Then reimagine some of the hurtful experiences from your life, trying to see what the offender could become if Jesus lived within him or her. Envision the choices that this person might have made if she or he would have followed the example of Jesus. Try to see the potential presence of Jesus in this person.

If this is too painful—if, for example, the offender was abusive—reverse your reimagining: Meditate on Isaiah 53:3–5, where the prophet describes Jesus as the suffering servant. Imagine Jesus in *your* place when you were hurt. Envision Jesus as the victim. Recognize that, on the cross, Jesus suffered the pain not only of your *sins* but also of your *sorrows*. You can give your longings for revenge to Him, because He has already carried the pain that provoked these longings in the first place.

Meditate on the True Force

"Revenge is sweet"—
    or so I heard.
So, Lord, if you happen to be
    in a lightning-hurling mood
    at this moment,
I could certainly
    come up with a list
    of potential targets.
Like the no-good kid who stole my friend's computer.
Like the church members who lied about me.
    (Not only do they lie;
    I don't think they tithe, either—
    promising targets there, Lord.)
Like murderers and
    child-molesters and
    embezzlers and
    all the other hooligans who don't quite
    measure up to Your standards.
Whew!
Anyone else You'd like to add
    to my list, God?
Anyone else who deserves
    an unexpected dosage
    of divine judgment?
Oh, yeah…
Yes, I suppose that would include me, too, wouldn't it?
No, I'd rather not see that lightning bolt quite yet.
Yes, I guess my time might be better spent
    changing my own life.

No, I don't suppose I'll be needing anything else right now.
Nothing except…

> *could You listen*
> *to one last prayer?*

"Lord, be merciful to me, a sinner.
Changing me could take awhile."

PART
THREE

"IMPOSSIBLE TO SEE,
THE FUTURE IS"

Experiencing Awe in the Unexpected

THE GALACTIC REPUBLIC teeters on the threshold of civil war. The phantom menace was once a fleeting shadow on a distant horizon. Now it has swollen into a deluge of darkness, driven by violence and fattened by greed. In the capital of the crumbling republic, three Jedi Masters discuss the situation with the Supreme Chancellor.

"Master Yoda," Chancellor Palpatine asks, "do you really think it will come to war?"

Yoda meditates for a few moments before confessing his own blindness. "Impossible to see, the future is," the Jedi Master admits. "The dark side clouds everything."

The Last Step into a Life of Awe

Even if galactic civil war hasn't topped your most recent list of concerns, I suspect that you can sense the wisdom in Yoda's words. Haven't you faced a circumstance that has forced you to admit, "Impossible to see, the future is"?

Remember when you thought your future was foolproof? Everything was planned perfectly. A college degree and a loving spouse. Two-point-five children in an upscale house. Your next exit would lead directly into the land of Happily Ever After.

That's when the unexpected arrives.

Your guidance counselor says, "You've been expelled."

Your boss says, "You're fired."

Your doctor says, "It's cancer."

Your accountant says, "You're bankrupt."

Your spouse says, "It's over."

And suddenly, the dark side clouds everything.

When darkness looms over your life like a raging thunderhead, you find yourself in the same situation as the Lord of

Creation, weeping amid the olive trees of Gethsemane (see Matthew 26:36–46); as the prophet Jeremiah, sobbing over his shattered homeland (see Lamentations 1); as Job cursing the day of his birth (see Job 3). You're struggling to carry a burden that you would never have chosen on your own.

At this point, you're faced with a crucial question: *Will I still live as if the larger world is the greatest reality of all, even when darkness clouds everything?*

When unexpected circumstances enshroud our pathway, it's difficult to trust that the larger world is still the greatest reality of all. Yet if we honestly long to live in awe in every present moment, this is precisely the sort of providence in which we *must* trust. Until that point, we are missing the greatest awe of all—the sense of wonder that saturates our souls when we realize that God's providential plan encompasses not only the events we expected but also the ones we could never have seen coming. Only then do we see that God is always working in our lives, integrating every unexpected event into His own perfect plan.

> *In all things God works for the good of those who love him, who have been called according to his purpose.*
>
> ROMANS 8:28

Good Catastrophes

J. R. R. Tolkien coined a wonderful word to describe unexpected events that a greater power turns into a grand master plan. Tolkien called such events *eucatastrophes* ("good catastrophes") and filled his timeless tales with them. Here's how Tolkien described the sense of awe that sweeps through us when we recognize that the catastrophes in a story were actually eucatastrophes:

> However wild its events, however fantastic or terrible the adventures, it can give to the child or man that hears it, when the "turn" comes, a catch of the breath, a beat and lifting of the heart, near to (or indeed accompanied by) tears, as keen as that given by any form of literary art.[1]

The *Star Wars* films never flinch from the fact that catastrophe frequently darkens the hero's path. Qui-Gon Jinn finds the chosen one but loses his life. Anakin Skywalker becomes a Jedi but loses his soul. Padmé Amidala finds the love of her life, only to die of a broken heart. The Jedi Knights discover the source of the phantom menace, only to be destroyed by one of their own.

At the same time, the *Star Wars* saga affirms that a greater power is always working, turning every catastrophe into eucatastrophe. Before the credits at the close of *Episode VI—Return of the Jedi*, it becomes clear that every catastrophe was a necessary step toward the climactic eucatastrophe that turns the saga's final moments from disaster to joy—Anakin Skywalker's decision to sacrifice his own life to redeem a fallen galaxy.

> eucatastrophe *n.* [yü-kə-′tas-tre-fē] 1. An unexpected event that a greater power weaves into a grand master plan. 2. In a fairy tale, the sudden happy turn that pierces the reader with unexpected joy. [2]

The best news about catastrophes and eucatastrophes is, however, far greater than anything you may feel while watching an epic film or reading a classic tale. The best news about eucatastrophe is that *this is how God really works*. God desperately longs to turn your catastrophes into eucatastrophes.

Don't get me wrong: I'm not promoting the foolish notion that everything that happens in your life is good. God has never promised that every event in your life would—or even *should*—be good. (This is, after all, the same deity whose own career culminated somewhere between an execution-stake and a borrowed tomb.) What God *has* promised is this: He is always working, even in your catastrophes, weaving every loose thread in your life into a lavish tapestry of eucatastrophes. "We can be…sure," the apostle Paul wrote, "that every detail in our lives…is worked into something good" (Romans 8:28, *The Message*).

God loves eucatastrophes.

The purpose of this section of *Finding God in a Galaxy Far, Far Away* is to help you to stand in awe even during the unexpected events of your life, during the dark moments of fear and shadows. Nothing can change the truth of Yoda's confession—"Impossible to see, the future is."

The Gospels contain…many marvels— peculiarly artistic, beautiful, and moving; and among the marvels is the greatest and most complete conceivable eucatastrophe… The Resurrection is the eucatastrophe of the story of the Incarnation… This story is supreme; and it is true.[3]

J. R. R. TOLKIEN

What *is* possible is to live in awe of the One who has already seen the future and who longs to twine every strand of our lives—even the dark and bitter fibers that we would prefer to forget—into a dazzling fabric that far outstrips our wildest fantasies.

"Afraid, Are You?"

"Train yourself to let go of everything you fear to lose."

YODA, JEDI MASTER
STAR WARS: EPISODE III—REVENGE OF THE SITH

"Do not be afraid, for I am with you."

GOD
ISAIAH 43:5

The setting sun splashes a golden glow across the parapets of the Jedi Temple. The temple's five spires stretch into the sky like the fingers of a massive hand, straining to stroke the surface of a larger world. For a thousand generations, these spires have spun their slender shadows across the streets and rooftops of Coruscant, silently signifying the Jedi Order's commitment to protect the Galactic Republic. In the upper chamber of the outermost spire, twelve Jedi Masters encircle the least likely of creatures.

A boy.

By all appearances, an ordinary humanoid.

Only a few days earlier, the boy was a slave laboring on a barren sphere in the galaxy's outer rim. Now the High Council has gathered to determine whether this child will become a

Jedi—and, more important, to discern whether he might be the long-awaited savior.

Centuries earlier, a prophet predicted the ascension of one who would bring balance to the Force. The Jedi expected the chosen one to be a cunning warrior, rising from their own ranks. But now...now Master Qui-Gon Jinn has claimed that this boy—this slave-child!—is the chosen one. The boy *is* special; no one on the council can deny that. But the *chosen one*? No one seems certain. No one but Qui-Gon.

And in time of greatest despair there shall come a savior and he shall be known as: THE SON OF THE SUN.

"ANCIENT PROPHECY" FROM *JOURNAL OF THE WHILLS,* AN EARLY DRAFT OF *STAR WARS* SAGA

"A bantha. A hyperdrive." Standing in the center of the council chamber, Anakin Skywalker cannot see the images that flash momentarily on one Jedi Master's view-screen. But he can sense them. Perfectly.

"A proton blaster. A Republic cruiser. A Rodian cup," Anakin's recitation continues. "A Hutt speeder."

Master Windu lays aside his view-screen and nods to Yoda. The Force runs strong in the boy.

"How feel you?" Yoda asks, his golden-green eyes searching the cherubic face before him.

"Cold, sir."

Uncertainty about the boy's future pricks at Yoda like a splinter in his soul. Something isn't right—and still, Yoda can feel the Force radiating powerfully from the child. Warm, familiar waves of energy wash over the ancient master, punctuated by lightning-like surges of...

"Afraid, are you?"

"No, sir," Anakin replies quickly, but it is too late. The council members already know better.

"Your thoughts dwell on your mother," another wizened Jedi master opines, forming each syllable carefully.

Yoda nods. "Afraid to lose her, I think."

Suddenly, the boy's disposition twists from innocence to defiance. The Jedi Master has needled a tender nerve.

"What has that got to do with anything?" Anakin snaps, eyes flashing.

"Everything!" Yoda's gaze cuts to the core of Anakin's rage. "Fear is the path to the dark side. Fear leads to anger. Anger leads to hate. *Hate* leads to suffering."

> *"Fear is the path to the dark side. Fear leads to anger. Anger leads to hate. Hate leads to suffering."*
>
> YODA, JEDI MASTER
> STAR WARS: EPISODE I—
> THE PHANTOM MENACE

The boy breathes deeply, groping for some sense of calm.

Yoda sighs. "I sense much fear in you."

You Were Not Fashioned to Live in Fear

"Afraid, are you?" Yoda asks, and each Jedi Master feels the fear that the child denies. Anakin Skywalker *is* afraid. What he fears most is that, if he surrenders his life to the Jedi Order, he will have to let go of his own hopes and dreams.

Anakin Skywalker never learns to restrain this fear. As a Padawan, his fear spawns darksome dreams of death and loss. When his mother dies in the deserts of Tatooine, his fear swells into anger, and he slaughters an entire community of Sand People. When foreboding nightmares about his spouse consume his soul in *Episode III—Revenge of the Sith*, it is fear that drives Anakin toward the dark side of the Force.

There's a vital truth to be learned from the fall of Anakin Skywalker. It's simply this: *You were not fashioned to live in fear.* That's why worry and stress cause such chaos in your life. Your Creator crafted your soul to flourish in faith, not to drown in fear.

E. Stanley Jones stated this truth with characteristic elegance:

> I am inwardly fashioned for faith, not for fear… I am so made that worry and anxiety are sand in the machinery of life; faith is the oil… In anxiety and worry, my being is gasping for breath—these are not my native air. But in faith and confidence, I breathe freely—these are my native air. A Johns Hopkins University doctor says, "We do not know why it is that worriers die sooner than non-worriers, but that is a fact." But I, who am simple of mind, think I know: We are inwardly constructed in nerve and tissue, brain cell and soul, for faith and not for fear. God made us that way.[1]

By focusing on forsaking one's fears, the *Star Wars* saga echoes a central theme of faith in Jesus. "Do not be afraid," the Lord commands nearly seventy times in the Scriptures.[2] In response to this command, the psalmist sang, "The LORD is my light and my salvation—whom shall I fear?" (Psalm 27:1). "Be strong, do not fear," Isaiah prophesied, "your God will come" (Isaiah 35:4). Later, the same prophet predicted a glorious future for God's people—a time when they "will have nothing to fear" (Isaiah 54:14).

Far More to Fear than Fear Itself

Let's be honest, though: Despite divine commands and prophetic predictions of a future life without fear, *we're all afraid of something*. The very phrase "primal fear" emerges from the fact that fear seems, well, *primal*—fear feels as if it's rooted in the primary essence of our beings.[3] And so, from womb to tomb, we work to free ourselves from fear. An entire line of sportswear has capitalized on our longing to be free from fear, each product proudly proclaiming the trait that none of us actually possesses: "No fear."

> We are inwardly constructed in nerve and tissue, brain cell and soul, for faith and not for fear. God made us that way.
>
> E. STANLEY JONES

Because fear is a universal fact of human life, fear is also a fundamental factor in every timeless myth and fairy tale. Skywalker and Kenobi, Neo and Trinity, Samwise and Frodo, Odysseus and Penelope—all of them fight not only visible foes but also invisible fears. In the myths of ancient Greece, the god of fear stood at the center of the shield of Heracles.[4] In the moments preceding the final battle for the kingdom of Narnia, it was said that "fear reigned over Narnia."[5] In the books of the Brothers Grimm, there's even a tale entitled "The Boy Who Went Forth to Find Fear."[6] The comic twist at the close of this fairy tale serves as a tacit reminder that most of us don't need to find fear; precisely when we least expect it, fear finds *us*.

The Longing for Control

If fear is so widespread, why does this phenomenon still wield such devastating power in people's lives? Why haven't we learned to cope with fear? To find out, let's look more closely at the inner workings of fear.

After more than a decade of pastoral dealings with people's hopes and fears, I am convinced that all fear flows from the same fountain: Fear arises when we realize that we are not in control. And, deep inside, each of us longs to be in control. That was the problem Anakin Skywalker faced. Do you recall his conversation with Padmé following the death of his mother?

ANAKIN: "Why couldn't I save her? I know I could have!"

PADMÉ: "Ani, you tried. Sometimes there are things no one can fix. You're not all-powerful."

ANAKIN: "But I should be! And someday I will be! I will be the most powerful Jedi ever!… I will even learn to stop people from dying!"

Anakin Skywalker craves power over the unexpected—even to the point of longing for control over life and death. So when the shape of his future slips from his hands, Anakin becomes afraid. In his fear, Anakin embraces darkness and rage not because he loves evil but because he longs for control. "I am one of the most powerful Jedi," Anakin whispers to his wife, moments before his fall to the dark side, "but I'm not satisfied… I want more."

The craving to control our destinies is as close as your own heart and as ancient as the human race. Slithering amid the leaves of Eden, the serpent whispered in the ear of Eve, "You will be like God" (Genesis 3:5)—in other words, "You can be in control." Brandishing a bloodied club over his brother's lifeless body, Cain experienced a fleeting rush of satisfaction because he felt—if only for an instant—as if he could control life and death (Genesis 4:1–12). Standing on the cornerstone of the Tower of

Babel, humanity cried out, "Let us build...a tower that reaches to the heavens, so that we may make a name for ourselves" (Genesis 11:4)—in other words, "Let's construct a monolith that puts us in control."

In every case, the primary players in these ancient dramas promptly discovered that they were not in control after all. As a result, they found themselves living in fear. The tongues of the tower builders became mysteriously twisted, and their confusion scattered them to the four winds (see Genesis 11:8–9). Cain found that, though he could wash his brother's blood from his hands, he could not cleanse the guilt from his heart, and his fear sent him fleeing to a far country (see Genesis 4:13–14). When God discovered Eve hiding beside her husband in the undergrowth of Eden, Adam offered a single rationale for running from his Maker: "I was afraid" (Genesis 3:10).

More often than I care to admit, I find myself following the same pattern as Eve and Cain and the builders of Babel: *I live under the arrogant delusion that I should be in control.* As a result, whenever unexpected events frustrate my intents, I become angry at my present circumstances and I fear for my future dreams. In the midst of my worries, I completely miss the gentle whisper of Jesus, saying, "Give your entire attention to what God is doing right now, and don't get worked up about what may or may not happen tomorrow. God will help you deal with whatever hard things come up when the time comes" (Matthew 6:34, *The Message*).

"Let Go of Everything You Fear to Lose"

So how do we learn to forsake our worries and fears? Or can we? When it comes to dealing with our worries, there's wisdom to be found in the words of Master Yoda. When Anakin Skywalker confesses his fears of the future, here's what the Jedi Master suggests:

YODA: "Careful you must be when sensing the future, Anakin.
    The fear of loss is a path to the dark side."
ANAKIN: "I won't let these visions come true, Master Yoda…
    What must I do?"
YODA: "Train yourself to let go of everything you fear to lose."

The first step on the pathway to forsaking your fears is *learning to let go of everything you're afraid to lose.*

Jesus made much the same point to His disciples a few days before He turned His face toward the cross. Jesus declared, "Anyone who comes to me but refuses to let go of father, mother, spouse, children, brothers, sisters—yes, even one's own self!— can't be my disciple" (Luke 14:26, *The Message*).[7] May I paraphrase the Messiah's message? "As long as you live in fear of losing what you love, you don't truly love me. So let go of everything you fear to lose. Then you'll be able to follow me."

> *"You can't stop change any more than you can stop the suns from setting."*
>
> SHMI SKYWALKER,
> ANAKIN'S MOTHER
> *STAR WARS: EPISODE I—
> THE PHANTOM MENACE*

This sort of "letting go" doesn't necessarily require you to forsake the people or the possessions that provide you with joy. It *does* require you to let go of the delusion that anything you call your own—whether people or properties, possessions or plans—actually belongs to you. It means recognizing everything in your life as the property of a power greater than your own. It means letting go of your lust for control.

Anakin Skywalker's downfall is his refusal to let go of his longing for control. He seethes at his present failures and fears for his future losses. And in the words of Master Yoda, "The fear of loss is a path to the dark side." For you and me, the situation is equally grievous—when we refuse to let go, we find ourselves stumbling down the dark paths of bitterness, anger, and stress. If you've spent time on those paths lately, perhaps it's time for *you* to learn to let go.

When I Finally Let Go

When I let go of my longing for control, nothing in my life can stay the same. I no longer fear losing my possessions, because I finally see that none of my belongings belongs to me anyway. I am only the temporary trustee of a tiny handful of *God's* belongings. That's why Jesus told His earliest followers, "Don't hesitate to let others use your possessions. If some of your belongings never find their way home, don't worry about it! They belonged to God anyway. If God needs them back, He can find them without your help."[8]

When I let go of my longing for control, I no longer live in fear of losing my family, because I see that they, too, belong to God. This recognition doesn't mean that I love my wife or my daughter any less. On the contrary, I love them *more*, because I see them for

> *"Anyone who comes to me but refuses to let go of father, mother, spouse, children, brothers, sisters—yes, even one's own self!—can't be my disciple."*
>
> JESUS
> LUKE 14:26, *THE MESSAGE*

111

The next hour, the next moment, is as much beyond our grasp and as much in God's care, as that a hundred years away. Worrying about the next minute is just as foolish as worrying about a day in the next thousand years— in neither case can we do anything, in both God is doing everything.[10]

GEORGE MACDONALD

what they truly are—exquisite expressions of divine grace, loaned to me from the very heart of God. Since I cannot control the length or terms of God's loan, I prize every moment with them as a gift from God.

When I choose to live in this way, my fears of the future begin to fade. I learn to view every event in my life— even the ones that threaten to thwart my precious plans—as the raw material that God will somehow work into His own glorious story. I learn to believe that if God shreds my beautiful game plan and leads me into a valley instead of a mountaintop, it is because He longs for me to discover *His* plan—a plan more beautiful than anything I could ever have fathomed.[9] I learn to see that God is constantly forming each shattered fragment of my life into a magnificent mosaic of grace.

Then, when I finally let go of everything I fear to lose, I feel what I have craved for so long—a vast cascade of awe, flowing through my soul, washing my fears away.

Learn to Live in Awe...

...by letting go of everything you
fear to lose.

SPIRITUAL EXERCISES FOR THE
SERIOUS PADAWAN

Be Mindful of the True Force

Carefully read Matthew 6:25–34. "Do not," Jesus commands in this passage, "worry about tomorrow." Are you honestly obeying these words? What causes fear and worry in your life? List your fears on a sheet of paper. Beside each fear, answer two questions: (1) *What am I really afraid of losing?* and (2) *How can I let go of what I fear to lose?* For example, if you fear death, your first answer might be, "I am afraid to lose my family—I don't know what would happen to them if I died." Your second response could be, "I can let go of my desire to be in charge of my family's future. I will entrust my family members to God. I will trust God to take care of them."

At the bottom of the page, copy 1 Peter 5:7 and Philippians 4:6–7. Commit yourself to memorize one of these passages this week. Whenever you feel worry or fear growing within you, recite the passage, claiming each phrase as a promise from God to you.

Meditate on the True Force

"Fear not."
Easy for You to say, Lord.
After all, what's ever happened
*   that could possibly make You afraid?*
I mean, besides the soldiers in the garden…
*   besides the thorns and the nails…*
*   besides the…*
Okay, I get it.
You had plenty to fear,
and yet You never worried
because You had already let go
*   of everything that You had the right to control.*
You let go of heaven—
*   released all the benefits of being God—*
*   simply so that*
*   You could always hold on to me.*

"The Lord is my light and my salvation—
*   whom shall I fear?"*
"The Lord is the stronghold of my life—
*   of whom shall I be afraid?"*

"When You Are Calm, at Peace"

LUKE SKYWALKER: *"But how am I to know the good side from the bad?"*
YODA: *"You will know. When you are calm, at peace."*
STAR WARS: EPISODE V—THE EMPIRE STRIKES BACK

"Peace I leave with you; my peace I give you… Do not let your hearts be troubled and do not be afraid."
JESUS
JOHN 14:27

Slender vines, enshrouded in a death-gray haze, dangle from distant treetops. Their tangled tendrils hint at the presence of sunlight somewhere past the upper layers of this swamp-ridden planet. Suddenly, something—humanoid, with a living burden belted to his back—bursts through the mist. He flings himself from one vine to another, sensing the living cells flowing through the pith of each vine long before his fingers seize the plant's slippery surface. Somersaulting in midair, the young Jedi lands on his feet and continues his dash through the undergrowth, deftly dodging mossy roots and rocks.

A casual observer might assume the young man to be an amazing athlete competing in an absurdly difficult race. But the wizened alien strapped across his shoulders knows better. The strength that surges within the young Jedi's body flows from a greater source—the power of a larger world.

"Run! Yes," Yoda whispers. "A Jedi's strength flows from the Force. But beware of the dark side. Anger...fear...aggression. The dark side of the Force are they. Easily they flow, quick to join you in a fight. If once you start down the dark path, forever will it dominate your destiny. Consume you it will."

Luke Skywalker halts, panting heavily, "But how am I to know the good side from the bad?"

"You will know. When you are calm, at peace. Passive. A Jedi uses the Force for knowledge and defense, never for attack." Yoda slips from his student's shoulders, landing gently on the sodden soil.

As Luke drapes his jacket across his back, a curious sensation seizes his attention. He turns toward the source of the disturbance and sees only the twisted roots of a tree, coiled like glistening serpents around the mouth of a cave...dead...yet somehow radiating darkness.

"There's something not right here." Luke's voice is filled with questions that he does not know the words to ask. "I feel cold, death."

"That place"—the master eyes his pupil carefully—"is strong with the dark side of the Force. A domain of evil it is. In you must go."

"What's in there?"

A moment of silence precedes the ancient Jedi's cryptic reply: "Only what you take with you." As Luke turns toward the cave, Yoda cautions him, "Your weapons...you will not need them."

Ignoring his master's counsel, Luke Skywalker gathers his weapons and clambers into the cavity beneath the tree. The cave walls are awash with a haunting cerulean hue. At first, Luke seems to be standing in an empty grotto—dank, dark, but unremarkable. Then, in the midst of a smoldering mist, he glimpses an unmistakable silhouette. It is his enemy...the Dark Lord of the Sith...the scourge of the Jedi Order ...Darth Vader.

Vader's blood-red blade blazes to life, and he raises his lightsaber to strike—but the younger Jedi is quicker. Luke's saber slashes across his enemy's shoulders, cleaving Vader's head from his body. The dark helmet reels along the floor of the cave before erupting in a shower of sparks. When the smoke clears, Luke sees that the face within the helmet is not Darth Vader's.

"Beware of the dark side. Anger...fear... aggression. The dark side of the Force are they. Easily they flow, quick to join you in a fight."

YODA, JEDI MASTER
STAR WARS: EPISODE V—
THE EMPIRE STRIKES BACK

It is his own.

Without warning, the helmet vanishes in a wisp of fog. Luke has lashed out at a dream.

Fashioned for Peace

"When you are calm, at peace," Yoda says to Luke. And to people caught in the maelstrom of a culture that cannot slow down, his words sound appealing. Wouldn't it be nice to find a place where calmness reigns supreme? A point at which your head stops throbbing, your heart stops pounding, and the joy of your present reality eclipses your fear of future difficulties? A place where peace abounds?

Throughout the *Star Wars* saga, peace is presented as an essential quality of the Jedi Knight. In the prequel trilogy, it is Anakin Skywalker's lack of inner peace that presses him toward the dark side of the Force. In the classic trilogy, calmness and peace are precisely the qualities that Yoda strives to produce in Luke Skywalker. This emphasis on peace appeals to us for the reason that, as children of the King, *we were created to live in peace*. Our Creator did not form our hearts merely to long for peace in some future time or place. God fashioned us to pitch our tents in the land of peace *here and now*.

The God of Israel repeatedly refers to His love for His people as a "covenant of peace" (Numbers 25:12; Isaiah 54:10; Ezekiel 34:25; 37:26; Malachi 2:5). His Messiah was dubbed "Prince of Peace" before he was even born (Isaiah 9:6). "Peace I leave with you" Jesus promised His disciples, "my peace I give you" (John 14:27). Looking into the faces of those who had rejected Him, Jesus wept for their lack of peace: "If you, even you," he cried out, "had only known on this day what would bring you peace" (Luke 19:42).

---

peace *n.* Inner sense of calmness and harmony with one's surroundings. Often represented by the Hebrew word *shalom* ("wholeness," "soundness," "well-being"). In the *Star Wars* saga, an essential quality of the Jedi Knights.

The Problem with Peace

Learning to experience God's peace is an essential part of learning to experience the full power of the larger world. The larger world is, after all, not only the foundation of our longings for wonder and awe, but also a fountain of peace. There's a problem with this peace, though: It's easy to dream about peace in some future time or place, but it's difficult to practice it here and now.

Practicing peace is difficult because *practicing peace requires us to deal with our own darkness.* That's what Luke Skywalker discovers on the planet Dagobah. Despite his best efforts to find peace, shadows from Luke's past still consume his soul. He yearns for the father whose face he has never seen, and he despises Darth Vader from the depths of his being. He is haunted by restlessness, recklessness, and impatience.

All of these shadows have mingled together within Luke's soul until there is, in Yoda's words, "Much anger in him, like his father." That's why, when Luke asks Yoda how to recognize the dark side of the Force, his teacher reminds him, "You will know. When you are calm, at peace." In other words, "Until you find peace within you, you will never be able to resist the darkness beyond you."

That's the central point of Luke Skywalker's ominous encounter in the cave. Crawling into the darkness with his hand resting on his weapons, Luke takes his own inner chaos with him. When he sees his own face in Darth Vader's helmet, he learns that the one he is destroying with his lack of peace isn't the Dark Lord of the Sith; it is himself. Before Luke can defeat the darkness of his enemy, he must first confront the shadows in himself.

So must you.

By choosing to pursue your yearnings for a larger world, you have set out on a hero's quest—an extraordinary journey into a wild and wonderful land. And in every hero's quest, the hero struggles against some dark inward specters—shadows that the hero must defeat to bring his quest to completion.[1]

When Odysseus descends into Hades, he faces not only the spirit of Tiresias but also sinister shades of his own making. When Frodo Baggins stumbles into the depths of Mordor, the hobbit battles not only the shadows of Sauron but also his own dark longings to keep the ring for himself. When Luke Skywalker drops into the cave beneath the tree, his real enemy isn't the shadowy Sith but the shadows within himself.

And before you can complete your quest for a larger world, you, too, will have to face some lingering shadows.

The shadow is our unconscious self, all the parts of ourselves that we refuse to acknowledge or are shamed by. The more we try to flee from or ignore the shadow, the more it grows and the more power it gains over us. To master the shadow, we need to stop running, turn, and face it.[2]

JODY G. BOWER

Dealing with Your Shadows

The shadows in your life don't typically converge into the shape of a Sith Lord, and you probably haven't lashed out at them with a lightsaber outside your dreams. Still, if the landscape of your life is anything like mine, it's littered with its share of shadowy caves and twisted trees. And these shadowed places are much deeper, much darker, and more subtle than anything Luke Skywalker ever experienced. They're the brutal word from a parent that still stings like a bitter slap; the unbroken habit that's about to break your heart; the inner discontent that causes you to buy the lie, "If only I can have *that*, I will be satisfied." They're the past regrets that persist in stealing the peace from our present realities.

Once we honestly recognize these dark specters, we find ourselves asking, *How can I move beyond these shadows? Or, can I? Is it really possible to live in peace in the present moment?* The best response I know is embedded in Yoda's counsel to Luke as the young Jedi slips into the cave beneath the tree. "Your weapons," Yoda warns, "you will not need them." Luke, reckless and impatient, refuses his master's counsel. As a result, he finds himself fighting against his own shadows again.

Whenever we struggle with ourselves, even when we win, we lose.

So how do you defeat your darkness once and for all? The solution is simple: *Leave your sword with the Master.* No, not with a pint-sized puppet in a swamp.

> *Surely he took up our infirmities and carried our sorrows... The punishment that brought us peace was upon him.*
> ISAIAH 53:4–5

Leave your sword with your *heavenly* Master. The One who fills the larger world with splendor and grace. The One who urges, "Come to me, all you who are weary and burdened, and I will give you rest" (Matthew 11:28). This Master knows your darkest shadows better than you know yourself. He has, after all, already carried them on the cross, where "He took on Himself our troubles and carried our sorrows... He was punished so we would have peace" (Isaiah 53:4–5, NLV).

Leaving Your Sword with the Master

Leaving your sword doesn't mean surrendering the plastic lightsaber that you keep in the closet. (You know the one, with the pulsating light and the real movie sound effects. You said it was for the kids, but everyone knows who *really* wanted it.) The swords you need to leave with the Master are far more deadly.

They're the *rage* that swells in your soul when you recall how deeply you were violated; the *fear* that chills your heart when you wonder what will happen if you fail to achieve your dreams; the *guilt* that gnaws at your gut each time you cry out, "My God, *why* did I do that?" The shades shift and the situations change from one person to another, but everyone has at least a few of these swords buried deep in the inner chambers of their hearts.

Over time, these emotions spawn deadly weapons. They erupt in the unexpected rage that clenches your chest, in the angry words that you hurl at your spouse, in the dark depression that binds you to your bed. You lash outward with these swords, trying desperately to destroy the shadows that have consumed your spirit and raped your soul. If this scenario describes you, what you're destroying isn't your darkness—it's yourself. You are sleeping with your own worst enemy on the nights when you sleep alone.

So what should you do? *Leave your sword with the Master.* Each time you sense the darkness seething and swelling within your soul, make this choice: "No longer will I lash out at my shadows in my own power. I will deal with my darkness by surrendering my weapons—my rage and anger, my guilt

All the broken and dislocated pieces of the universe—people and things, animals and atoms—get properly fixed and fit together in vibrant harmonies, all because of his death, his blood that poured down from the Cross.

COLOSSIANS 1:20,
THE MESSAGE

and shame—to my Master. I leave my sword with Him."

Leaving our swords with the Master isn't easy. After gripping these weapons for years, we suddenly feel vulnerable without them. But then we're forced to remember someone else who released His power—someone who "did not consider equality with God something to be grasped, but made himself nothing, taking the very nature of a servant" (Philippians 2:6). In the very moment when He could have called on twelve legions of angelic swords, He chose to let go of these swords instead (Matthew 26:53). In this way, He became broken and vulnerable for me and for you. And thus, brokenness and vulnerability became the means that the Master uses to lead us into a life of peace—which is to say, to lead us into *Himself*, "for he himself is our peace" (Ephesians 2:14).

What Happens When You Let Go

Near the end of the *Star Wars* saga, Luke Skywalker does find peace—but not until he lets go of his sword. Remember the climactic scene in *Episode VI—Return of the Jedi*? Anger and rage swell within Luke Skywalker as he battles Darth Vader, driving Luke closer and closer to the dark side of the Force. Finally, Luke Skywalker sees the opportunity that he has awaited for so long: Darth Vader is helpless as Luke's blade blazes less than an inch from the Sith Lord's throat.

"Good! Your hate has made you powerful," the Emperor cackles with glee. "Now, fulfill your destiny and take your father's place at my side."

Precious seconds slip by before Luke turns to face the dark Emperor. As he turns, he hurls his lightsaber away.

Once Luke Skywalker releases his weapon, he becomes

free—free from his rage, free from his darkness, free from his fear. In the Skywalkers' saga, this choice not only liberates Luke from his shadows but also leads to Anakin Skywalker's salvation.

In the saga of your life, releasing your sword produces something even greater—the inner sense of well-being that your soul has been searching for. It's what the apostle Paul described as "the peace of God, which transcends all understanding" (Philippians 4:7).

Finding Peace in the Midst of Pain

In everything, by prayer and petition, with thanksgiving, present your requests to God. And the peace of God, which transcends all understanding, will guard your hearts and your minds.

PHILIPPIANS 4:6–7

May I share with you how I learned to leave my sword with the Master? I didn't arrive at these conclusions through hours of reflection in some distant ivory tower. And as much as I enjoy going to the movies, I didn't find them there either. No, these conclusions came in the midst of a deep personal struggle to find peace at a time when peace had eluded my grasp.

In a single year, my wife and I endured the anguish of learning that we could not have biological children, coupled with three failed adoptions. Three times, the birth mothers changed their minds—once before the baby was born and twice afterward. I don't remember everything I said after the third birth mother reneged, but I do know this: I wielded my pain like a weapon—a dark, raging sword that I directed at the birth mothers, at myself, even at God.

It was somewhere in the midst of these months of weltering and wailing that a new prospect emerged. A family in another state had adopted a Romanian orphan and then abandoned her. Would we be interested in an older child? Mounds of paperwork alternated with manic preparation and, six months later, we found ourselves standing in a judge's chambers, declaring ourselves to be the parents of a spunky seven-year-old girl named Hannah.

On the way home that evening, we saw the setting sun spin a fiery kaleidoscope across the western sky. Lustrous clouds formed a canopy under which the spiritual and the material realms frolicked with one another like brazen newlyweds, flirting and swirling, twirling and finally tumbling together into a bed as broad as the cosmos.

"God sure made a pretty sky tonight, didn't He?" I said.

"Mm-hmm," a sleepy voice from the backseat replied. Hannah curled up against a pink pillow, and there was a long silence. Suddenly, Hannah sat up.

"Daddy, know what? God put red in the sky tonight—that's Mommy's favorite color. There's blue for you. Over there is pink; that's for me."

> *When we become aware that we do not have to escape our pains, but that we can mobilize them into a common search for life, those very pains are transformed from expressions of despair into signs of hope.*[3]
>
> HENRI J. M. NOUWEN

"There are colors in the sky tonight for everyone in our family, aren't there?"

"Uh-huh. Know what else, Daddy? I think God's happy tonight, because He's finally gotten all the colors together. How 'bout you?"

Several moments passed before a reply wedged its way past the lump in my throat.

"Yes, Hannah. I'm happy, too," I said. "I'm happy, too."

It was there—somewhere between the innocent observation of my daughter and the luminous wonder of a western sunset—that the swords of bitterness and rage finally slipped from my hands. And the peace of God began to seep, ever so slowly, back into the scarred recesses of my soul.

My difficulty in those months didn't have to do with the availability of God's peace or even with God's desire to respond to my prayers. God had in fact prepared His response long before I whispered my first prayer for a child. The problem was that I had refused to leave my sword with the Master.

> *Lord, make me an instrument of your peace… For it is in giving that we receive, it is in pardoning that we receive pardon, and it is in dying that we are born to eternal life.*
>
> TRADITIONAL PRAYER OF ST. FRANCIS OF ASSISI

And the only foe I was destroying was myself.

Free from the Shadows

This is, I see now, how God most often weaves peace into His children's lives: As in the most magnificent of sunsets, God whirls together hues and shades in our lives that no interior decorator would dream of combining. Somehow, the shades that we had planned don't quite make it onto the Master Artist's palette, and in our moments of impatience His selections can seem dubious at best. Then one day, when you finally release your weapons, you see the truth: The very circumstances you questioned and even cursed were part of a peace that God was forming long before you even knew the words to make your request.

That's when you step into the fullest experience of the larger world.

This is not to say that you'll never experience another shadow; you'll still deal with your share of dark moments. But the shadow's stranglehold on your soul has been shattered, and you are free—free to ignore the commercials that correlate your happiness with your buying habits; free to rejoice in the hints of your Savior's presence in every part of your life; free to gaze into the heavens, to feel the gentle caress of God's Spirit, and to sing into the wind, "My soul rejoices in my God. For he has clothed me with garments of salvation" (Isaiah 61:10). Finally, you are free to stand in awe.

Learn to Live in Awe...

...by leaving your sword with the Master.

SPIRITUAL EXERCISES FOR THE SERIOUS PADAWAN

Be Mindful of the True Force

Make an honest assessment of the shadows in your life. List them on a sheet of paper. Ask yourself, "Which of these shadows am I still fighting?" Select a song to guide you as you seek a new sense of peace during this week—perhaps a classic hymn such as "It Is Well with My Soul." Schedule opportunities during the week to meditate on several Scriptures such as Psalm 55:22, Matthew 11:28–30, 1 Peter 5:7, and especially Philippians 4:4–9. During these moments of meditation, take the time to find inner quiet and calmness. Be honest with yourself about the shadows in your life. Take time to recognize each one. When you are ready, slowly release each shadow, each inner conflict that steals your joy. If necessary, be willing to enlist the assistance of a pastor or counselor to help you make your way into the land of peace.

Meditate on the True Force

"Lord, make me an instrument of Your peace"—
it's a beautiful sentiment
but a difficult quest.
Especially when there are
so many dirty corners in my heart,
> *so many dark shadows,*
> *so many swords and scars*
> *that only You can see.*
Please let me live a life of peace—
a life in which I let go of everything,
> *everything that shackles me to yesterday,*
> *everything that imprisons me in my small self today,*
> *everything that terrifies me*
> *with the uncertainty of tomorrow.*
Everything except You.
Please let me find my peace in You—
> *because then (and only then) am I free.*
And, oh, how I long to live free.

Epic Possibilities in Unexpected Places

LUKE: *"You're coming with me... I've got to save you."*
ANAKIN: *"You already have, Luke... You were right about me."*
STAR WARS: EPISODE VI: RETURN OF THE JEDI

"If anyone would come after me, he must deny himself and take up his cross and follow me. For whoever wants to save his life will lose it, but whoever loses his life for me will find it."

JESUS
MATTHEW 16:24

o!" the young Jedi roars.

Emerald flame blazes from the handle of the Jedi's lightsaber. He leaps toward the Sith Lord, slashing wildly, but his enemy's blade is already prepared. Their swords sputter against one another, showering Jedi and Sith in multi-hued sparks.

Rage spills like molten lava from the Jedi's every movement. He longs for nothing less than the Sith Lord's destruction—it is for this that he fights. And, yet, in his passion to destroy the Sith, the Jedi is dancing with the dark side of the Force—and the darkness is making him powerful. Still, somehow...Luke Skywalker also longs to save whatever fragment of goodness may remain within the Sith's black armor.

The Sith Lord senses this conflict, for he has faced it, too.

Before the dark times.

Before the empire.

Before a duel along the magma rivers of Mustafar reduced him to a charred scrap of humanity, trapped in this sinister fusion of man and machine.

Before he became Darth Vader.

Deep within, Darth Vader knows that he is no match for Luke Skywalker—or perhaps he is more than a match, and he simply longs for his son to join him in his darkness. Or perhaps...perhaps the conflict is not only in his son but also in himself. Maybe the grip of the dark side is failing and the fallen angel is longing for the light.

Luke's furious assault forces his father to his knees, and the emerald blade finally finds its mark, slashing through Darth Vader's wrist. Vader's hand plummets down a bottomless ventilation shaft, still clutching his crimson saber.

This is the moment that Luke Skywalker has craved for so long.

His enemy, the vile creature that was once his father, is at his mercy.

One stroke.

One stroke is all that it will take to end Darth Vader's life.

"Good!" Emperor Palpatine cackles. "Your hate has made you powerful. Now, fulfill your destiny and take your father's place at my side."

Just one stroke.

The young Jedi stares at the seared wires that dangle from Darth Vader's wrist, the remains of the hand that he has severed. As his father gasps for breath, Luke's eyes wander to his own black-gloved hand—a mechanical surrogate for the hand that Vader

severed in their last encounter. In this moment, Luke tastes the bitter truth: He is about to become the very thing that he hates.

One stroke is all that it would take for Darth Vader's life to
end—and for Luke Skywalker's darkness to begin.

Luke turns to face the dark Emperor.

"Never!" Luke pitches his lightsaber aside. "I'll never turn to
the dark side… I am a Jedi, like my father before me." The
young Jedi stands before the Emperor, utterly defenseless. He is
ready to die. And—precisely because he is ready to die—he is,
for the first time in his life, truly alive.

The Emperor's expression twists from glee to rage.

"So be it…Jedi," Palpatine hisses. "If you will not be turned,
you will be destroyed."

Cerulean lightning leaps from the Emperor's fingertips. The
first burst of lightning flings Luke to the floor. Then the burning
begins…dark blazes tearing like wildfire through the young
Skywalker's flesh. Luke can no longer see the Emperor, but he
feels the darksome shadow, and he hears the snarling voice.

"Young fool. Only now, at the end, do you understand," the
dark-robed shadow sneers. "Your feeble skills are no match for
the power of the dark side."

The bolts of lightning intensify, searing to the very bowels of
Luke's being. The young Jedi shrieks in anguish. He knows no
power—not even in the deepest mysteries of the Force—that
can stop this onslaught.

No power except, perhaps, the power of love.

"Father, please," Luke Skywalker screams. "Help me."

Darth Vader does not move.

"Now, young Skywalker"—the Emperor has tired of his tor-
turous game; he is ready to watch the last remnants of life seep
from Luke's flesh—"you will die."

A final gale of lightning erupts from the Emperor's hands, hurling Luke Skywalker into the wall. Darth Vader's gaze shifts from his son to the Emperor…to his son…the Emperor…his son.

Without warning, Vader seizes his master. The emperor howls in astonished rage. Lightning arcs uncontrollably across the observation deck, piercing Vader's breastplate and helmet. With one final burst of energy, Darth Vader hurls Emperor Palpatine from the deck into the bottomless pit.

Luke Skywalker and the black-armored warrior stare at each other in dazed reverie. The Sith menace has faded. The Force has fallen into balance. Salvation has arrived on a path that no one expected.

Anakin Skywalker lives again.

Moments later, Luke finds himself cradling his wounded father in his arms. Darth Vader's mechanical lungs are fighting for each shallow breath. The Dark Lord of the Sith is about to die.

> *"I can't kill my own father… There is still good in him."*
>
> LUKE SKYWALKER,
> JEDI KNIGHT
> *STAR WARS: EPISODE VI—
> RETURN OF THE JEDI*

"Luke," Anakin rasps, "help me take this mask off… Just for once…let me look on you with my own eyes."

Slowly, reverently, Luke detaches the dark façade from his father's face. The young Jedi's fingers are eager, but his eyes are anxious. Finally, the mask topples away. The face beneath is that of an old man, disfigured by flames and blanched by darkness.

Anakin Skywalker struggles to lift the corners of his mouth. He has not smiled in so many years. Not since those few seconds before Obi-Wan left Coruscant to fight the general of the droid armies, before Anakin's free fall into the darkness. If only

Obi-Wan could be here now…and Padmé. His precious Padmé.

Anakin feels the spring rains of Naboo trickling down his scarred face. He tastes the droplets of rain and realizes that they are not rain after all. They are tears—tears of regret and tears of joy, his son's and his own, mingling along his cracked lips. He loves this earnest boy who kneels before him. Once again, after these decades of darkness, he *loves*.

"Now…go, my son," the chosen one chokes. "Leave me."

"No," Luke protests. "You're coming with me… I've got to save you."

Anakin Skywalker's lips strain to form the self-assured grin that, once upon a time, the entire galaxy recognized and a certain senator from Naboo adored.

"You already have, Luke."

The Unexpected Twist

It's a trademark of every timeless tale: Before the closing credits roll, there's always a catastrophic twist that seems to turn the quest to tragedy. The White Witch's blade takes Aslan's life as he lies on the table of stone. Gandalf falls in the Balrog's lair, deep in the Morian mines. The Beast's last breath slips away before Belle declares her love. Luke Skywalker surrenders his sword and suffers the emperor's rage.

This tragic twist always seems to ensure the hero's defeat. Yet in every classic tale, an unexpected turn suddenly transforms the twist to victory: The Deeper Magic from before the Dawn of Time draws Aslan back to life. Gandalf the Grey returns to Middle-Earth in the glory of Gandalf the White. The kiss of Belle and her confession of love save the Beast from death. Salvation arrives on a pathway that no one ever expected.

Finding God in a Galaxy Far, Far Away

That's what happens in the closing moments of *Episode VI—Return of the Jedi*. Who could have expected that the climactic choice in the final episode would be the Jedi's decision to throw his lightsaber away? ("This weapon," the Jedi Masters repeatedly reminded their Padawans whenever a lightsaber was lost, "is your *life*.") Who would have guessed that Luke's cries of agony might move the arch-villain to sacrifice himself to save his son? And who could *ever* have fathomed that Luke's final encounter with Darth Vader would end not with the flashing of lightsabers but with the fledgling Jedi Knight cradling his father in his arms?

> *"Father, please.*
> *Help me."*
> LUKE SKYWALKER,
> JEDI KNIGHT
> *STAR WARS: EPISODE VI—*
> *RETURN OF THE JEDI*

At first glance, each of these twists seems to guarantee Luke's defeat. After all, what else could be the result of Luke Skywalker discarding his sword? Of crying to a Sith Lord for help? Of offering compassion to Darth Vader? And yet, each choice was a stepping-stone toward an experience of salvation that no one expected—the redemption of Anakin Skywalker.

You Were Made with a Hero's Heart

At their best, these unexpected turns from tragedy to victory inspire a profound sense of awe in us, swelling upward from our inmost beings—"a catch of the breath, a beat and lifting of the heart, near to (or indeed accompanied by) tears."[2] You know firsthand the feeling that I'm talking about: It's that moment, in the final chapters of a great book or movie, when you simultaneously feel a song in your heart and a lump in your throat—and perhaps even a trickle on your cheek.

135

When you experience this sort of awe, your first inclination is to swallow the lump in your throat and swab the wetness from your eyes, hoping that no one noticed your moment of weakness. After all, it's just a *story*, isn't it? Yet when you wipe away your tears, you risk wiping away with them a vital truth: The twists of the timeless tales ring true within you because they are the distant echoes of the story for which your soul was formed.

The black moment is the moment when the real message of transformation is going to come. At the darkest moment comes the light... At the bottom of the abyss comes the voice of salvation.[1]

JOSEPH CAMPBELL

So far, in this exploration of the *Star Wars* saga, you've learned to live in awe by embracing the wonders of a larger world, by delighting in the presence of God among His people, and by sensing the tracings of God's fingertips in the unexpected events of your life. Now it's time for the final step.

It's time for you to join God's story.

Yes, that's right—*you*.

You were formed to be far more than a footnote in some other person's story; you were made for a life of awe.

You were created to be part of an epic quest—a sweeping story far greater than anything the Jedi Council ever imagined.

You were fashioned for a story in which salvation always seems to show up on a pathway that no one ever expected.

You were made with a hero's heart.

That's why you feel that fleeting sense of awe whenever you hear the timeless tales. It's as if you've unexpectedly caught the familiar scent of a flower whose petals you've never touched, the latest news from a birthplace whose borders you've never crossed, the distant melody of a well-known tune that you've never heard before.[3] In these moments, you are experiencing a hint of the story for which you were created—*the story of God.*

Every timeless myth and fairy tale is "a splintered fragment" of God's story.[4] Every unexpected hero is a distant echo of the virgin-born boy from Galilee; every sacrificial twist is a whisper of the Cross; and every triumphant turn to victory is a misty reflection of the Resurrection.

> *Story and metaphor are at the heart of spirituality.*[6]
>
> LEONARD I. SWEET

We do not create myths merely to entertain ourselves; we tell these tales because—even in the moments when we deny it—we yearn to be part of the story for which we were created.[5]

Echoes of God's Story

So how can you join God's story? "You must," Yoda says as he trains Luke Skywalker on Dagobah, "unlearn what you have learned." It's good advice for a budding Jedi Knight. It's also good advice for taking your first steps into the full power of the story of God.

Deep inside, most of us believe that victory comes from human power; after all, from the perspective of our world, the most powerful people are those who are strong and in control. To experience the full power of God's story, however, you must unlearn what you have learned about power and victory.

In God's story—as in the finest of fairy tales—mere children can fell the mightiest giants, losers can turn out to be saviors, and shepherd boys can turn into kings (see 1 Samuel 16:1–18:7). In God's story, redeemers show up in precisely the places where no one ever suspected—in the deserts of Sinai, in the wilderness of Judea, in a feed trough in Bethlehem amid the steaming dung of sheep and goats (see Exodus 3:1; Matthew 3:1; Luke 2:1–7).

The only two things that can satisfy a soul are a person and a story.[7]

G. K. CHESTERTON

In God's story, heroes don't have to be powerful; they simply have to be available. Perhaps most surprising of all, in God's story the supreme episodes of salvation do not arrive by means of clashing armies and clanging swords; salvation slips into our lives in the moments when we least expect it, concealed in the modest garments of stillness and sacrifice. God's kingdom is, Jesus claimed, "like treasure hidden" (Matthew 13:44).

Like a beautiful enchantress wrapped in a beggar's rags.

Or a handsome prince disguised as a frog.

Or the salvation of the galaxy concealed in a farm boy from Tatooine.

All of them, distant echoes of the Savior of the universe, veiled in human flesh, struggling down the pathway that no one expected Him to take—the pathway to the cross.

The difference, of course, is that the story of the crucified Savior truly happened. Of all the timeless stories that have been told, "this story is supreme; and it is true."[8] To entrust your life to this story is to take your first tentative steps into the epic of God. For in this story, God divulged the divine truth of which the fairy tales are distant echoes: God's kingdom is a kingdom upside down—a kingdom where losers become winners, where the weak become strong, and where the meek inherit the earth.

Looking for the Possibilities

The finest of the timeless myths and fairy tales follow the essential patterns of God's story—they present us with a realm where the meek unexpectedly become mighty and the weak become strong. The *Star Wars* trilogies are no exception. When Obi-Wan Kenobi first hears about Anakin Skywalker in *Episode I—The Phantom Menace*, he senses only "another pathetic life-form," but Qui-Gon Jinn sees someone whose life is saturated with the Force. Everyone else sees a bothersome klutz when they bump into Jar-Jar Binks—or, perhaps more precisely, when *he* bumps into *them*—but Queen Amidala sees someone who can bring two estranged species together to overcome an extraterrestrial invasion. Everyone else sees a reckless teenager when they look at Luke Skywalker, but Obi-Wan Kenobi recognizes the hope of the galaxy.

In the final installment of the *Star Wars* saga, the specter of Obi-Wan sees the death of Darth Vader as the sole path to peace in the universe. Yet in precisely the place where the Jedi Master sees only difficulty, Luke sees possibility: Luke Skywalker believes that even the epitome of evil may yet repent. In every case, the difference between the hero and the rest

Who would have guessed that Israel of all nations would be the one God picked or Sarah would have Isaac at the age of ninety or the Messiah would turn up in a manger? Who could possibly see the duck-billed platypus coming or Saint Simeon Stylites or the character currently occupying the pulpit at First Presbyterian? The laugh in each case results from astonished delight at the sheer unexpectedness of the thing.[9]

FREDERICK BUECHNER

of the world is simply this: The hero sees possibilities in the places where others see difficulties.

Epic Possibilities in Each Present Moment

So how do we locate the epic possibilities in the midst of our day-to-day lives? The answer may be summarized in a single word: *look*. In every second of your life, epic possibilities already surround you. The question is whether you're willing to look long enough to trust in them. The Jedi Masters refer to this habit as being "mindful of the living Force"—as being aware of the epic possibilities that are available in each present moment.

> *God chose the foolish things of the world to shame the wise; God chose the weak things of the world to shame the strong.*
>
> 1 CORINTHIANS 1:27

Isn't this, after all, how Jesus lived? Jesus lived believing that His daily life was alive with epic possibilities. As a result, He looked at lilies and sparrows and saw signs of His Father's love (see Matthew 6:25–34). He looked at a woman whose romantic record was less than lustrous—five times divorced and currently enjoying a fling with a man who had no plans to buy a wedding ring—and saw an evangelist (see John 4:1–42). Most amazing of all, He saw epic possibilities in this sin-shattered planet, and it cost Him more than comfort and convenience. It cost Him heaven itself, and it sent Him all the way to the cross. And still, Jesus looked toward that bloody stake, plunged like a dagger into the heart of Mount Calvary, and saw the glory of God (see John 13:23–33).

What's more, Jesus expects everyone who joins His story to imitate His example. Remember Jesus' words to His first followers? "If anyone would come after me, he must deny himself and take up his cross daily and follow me. For whoever wants to save his life will lose it, but whoever loses his life for me will save it" (Luke 9:23–24). In other words, "If you want to join God's story, you must be willing to follow the plotline of God's story as far as I did— even to the point of seeing epic possibilities in a cross." In this way, Jesus reminded us that the true hero's quest lies not in creating new possibilities for tomorrow but in seeing today's possibilities with new eyes.

> *A mystic is someone who is awake to the voice that everyone hears.*[10]
>
> LEONARD I. SWEET

What if you spent every moment as Jesus did, looking for epic possibilities? What would you see? What about the child in your church whose hygienic habits leave much to be desired? Seen through the eyes of Jesus, perhaps she's a future missionary searching for someone willing to listen to her dreams. And the lonely stranger who always needs to talk precisely when you need to leave? Maybe he's a messenger from the throne of God, an angel of heaven in an Old Navy sweatshirt and threadbare shoes (see Hebrews 13:2). And all the people from whom you'd prefer to turn away—"the poor, the crippled, the blind and the lame" (Luke 14:21)? Perhaps they are signposts of God's kingdom, epic possibilities shrouded in veils of human flesh.

Inasmuch as you see divine possibilities where the rest of the world sees only difficulties and trivialities, you are a hero. It may not be the sort of heroism that will get your accomplishments recorded on a Jedi holocron. In truth, it's even better: It's the sort of heroism that enfolds your everyday life in a story that's far larger than yourself—the story of God.

The Great Story

Learning to look for epic possibilities doesn't mean that exhilarating adventures will suddenly supplant every mundane task in your life. Even when you live fully in God's story, the gas tank will still get empty, the baby's diaper will still get full, and the alarm clock's unearthly howl will still shatter your Monday morning slumber. Simply put, you won't always *feel* heroic when you're living in God's story.

Looking for epic possibilities is, after all, costly. Luke Skywalker believes in the possibility of his father's redemption—and finds himself thrashing in agony on the deck of the Death Star. Moments later, Darth Vader sees the possibility of saving the life of his son—and ends up facing death himself. To look for epic possibilities is to become *vulnerable*. It's true in the lands of our heroes' quests, and it's true here and now in *your* quest.

And yet, the resurrection of Jesus demonstrates that no tragic twist—not even a twist as apparently tragic as the cross—can bring God's story to an end. Once again, the story of God, like the finest of fairy tales, finds salvation in precisely the place that no one expected—in a tomb. The church father John Chrysostom told the story of this unexpected turn in a hymn:

> Hell took a body, and discovered God.
>> Hell took earth, and encountered heav'n.
> Death took what it saw, only to be
>> crushed by what it could not see.

Oh Death, oh Death, where is your sting?
    And, Hell, where is your victory?
Christ is Risen, angels elated!
    Christ is Risen, life's liberated!
Christ is Risen, indeed![11]

By delighting in His creation, God hallowed our world. By delighting in stories, God hallowed our timeless tales. By embracing the cross, God hallowed our sorrows. By bursting forth from an empty tomb, God proved that no story, no sorrow—nothing in all of creation, in fact—could ever stand in the way of His love.

Where the Road Goes Ever On

Despite our desire for the great stories to go on forever, every timeless tale has to end. The *Star Wars* saga is no different. No matter how many sequels, prequels, spin-offs, and spoofs that George Lucas and his heirs may allow, the story can't go on forever. The story that inspired such awe in me so many years ago will eventually end.

What's timeless about the timeless tales is not the tales themselves but the divine story that the tales reflect. The story of God, unlike every other quest and tale, lacks the page that proclaims "The End."

In fact, as C. S. Lewis hints in *The Chronicles of Narnia*, our full enjoyment of God's story doesn't even *begin* until the page that we think is the end—the paragraphs that we describe as "death" or "the end of time." In the final paragraphs of *The Last Battle*, as the full awareness of a larger world dawns on the creatures of Narnia, C. S. Lewis writes:

For them it was only the beginning of the real story. All their life in this world and all their adventures in Narnia had only been the cover and title page: now at last they were beginning Chapter One of the Great Story, which no one on earth has read: which goes on for ever: in which every chapter is better than the one before.[12]

Deep within, this is what we long for—a sense of awe that never stops growing, a road that "goes ever on and on,"[13] a story that's missing the page that says "The End."

So the children plunge into eternal bliss along Narnia's rolling knolls. King Arthur drifts into the ocean surrounded by a trio of queens. Bilbo and Frodo sail to the unknown West, where elven hosts live in eternal light. And the shimmering specters of the Jedi Knights, smiling and celebrating with Luke, flood the closing seconds of *Episode VI—Return of the Jedi* with unexpected joy. All of them are distant echoes of our desire to share in God's story, the One True Story that began before the beginning and that never has to end.

Learn to Live in Awe...

...by seeing the epic possibilities that fill every moment of your life.

SPIRITUAL EXERCISES FOR THE SERIOUS PADAWAN

Be Mindful of the True Force

Where do you struggle to see epic possibilities? What causes you to lose sight of the possibilities that are present in every moment of your life? List some of your struggles. Beside each struggle, answer this question: "The next time I face this person or situation, what epic possibility can I look for?" Study the following Scriptures—Matthew 9:9; Luke 23:39–43; and Acts 9:1–27. How does each Scripture demonstrate seeing an epic possibility in an unexpected person or place? How can these passages encourage you to look for epic possibilities in the situations you've listed?

Meditate on the True Force

Lord, I have a great idea:
Be more selective about where
You expect me to see
epic possibilities.
I'm having a tough time seeing anything epic
*   in hotheaded church members,*
*   in hygienically challenged children,*
*   in the excessively amorous homosexual couple*
*   sitting two booths away from me*
*   in a downtown restaurant.*
Just for a moment, Lord,
could You let me be
a bit more selective
about these possibilities?

I prefer people
    who are laid-back,
    well-groomed, and whose
    orientations match mine.
But if I claim to be
    part of Your story,
I can't be selective
    about these possibilities.
After all,
You weren't selective
about where You looked
for epic possibilities.
If You had been,
    You would never
    have selected
    me.

Earthbound Echoes of Heavenly Truth

The stories that seem immortal—The Oddysey, Don Quixote, David Copperfield, Huckleberry Finn—are all the same: A brave but flawed hero, a quest, colorful people and places, sidekicks, the discovery of life's underlying truths. If I were asked to say with certainty which movies will still be widely known a century or two from now, I would list 2001 *and* The Wizard of Oz, *and Keaton and Chaplin, and Astaire and Rogers, and probably* Casablanca, *and* Star Wars, *for sure.*[1]

ROGER EBERT

H ow quickly do we grow accustomed to wonders," Roger Ebert wrote in his review of *Star Wars: Episode I— The Phantom Menace.*

I am reminded of the Isaac Asimov story "Nightfall," about the planet where the stars were visible only once in a thousand years. So awesome was the sight that it drove men mad. We who can see the stars every night glance up casually at the cosmos and then quickly down again, searching for a Dairy Queen.[2]

For all the failures of the *Star Wars* saga—most notably the 1978 *Star Wars Holiday Special* that even my preschool self found impossible to endure—this franchise of fantasy films is filled with wonder and awe. "George Lucas," Ebert writes, "doesn't share the prevailing view that the future is a dark and lonely place. What he does have, in abundance, is exhilaration." [3]

As you've perused these pages, I hope that you've savored at least a few morsels of this exhilaration. But I hope you've sensed something more than the fleeting exhilaration of George Lucas. My vision is for you to drink deeply of the eternal exhilaration and awe of *God*.

At their best, the *Star Wars* movies may be seen as something like the moon that orbits our own planet—as an awe-inspiring reflection of the Source of Light, but a reflection nonetheless. The *Star Wars* films do not convey the truth; they are earthbound echoes of heavenly truth, pale reflections of the One True Story. Alone, these reflections offer us nothing more than a fleeting glance upward, a brief reprieve from the dim routines of our daily lives. And yet, if we allow these reflections to guide us toward the Source of Light, they can become parables of One True Story—the eternal story of God's love—and inspire us to look far beyond the stars themselves into the One who first swirled the suns and stars alike into existence.

Appendix

A Whirlwind Guide to the "Star Wars" Saga

If you are already familiar with the basic story line that draws the *Star Wars* trilogies together, don't read this section—dive directly into chapter 1! But maybe it's been awhile since you took a trip through George Lucas's space opera. Or perhaps you're a fresh fan of the films. If so, this summary of the *Star Wars* saga should help you as you plot a course through *Finding God in a Galaxy Far, Far Away*.

Star Wars: Episode I—The Phantom Menace (1999)

The first prequel introduces Anakin Skywalker as a nine-year-old slave with an extraordinary sensitivity to the Force.

An Imbalance in the Force
A long time ago in a galaxy far, far away, the Galactic Republic functioned as a peaceful partnership of planets and people, drawing together thousands of star systems and species into a single alliance. The primary guardians of this system were the

Jedi—an order of peacekeepers bound together by their devotion to "the Force," a mystical energy field that binds the universe together.

Following a millennium of peace and harmony, an elusive imbalance emerged in the Force. Little did the Jedi Knights know that this marked the rebirth of the Sith, an ancient order of warriors who used the Force for personal power rather than knowledge and defense.

In the midst of this tide of darkness, a Jedi Master named Qui-Gon Jinn encountered a nine-year-old slave on the planet Tatooine. Even as a slave, Anakin Skywalker demonstrated not only uncanny mechanical skills—having built a robot and a pod racer from castoff parts—but also an extraordinary sensitivity to the Force. Long ago, the prophets had predicted the birth of one who would bring balance to the Force. Convinced that this child was the fulfillment of the ancient prophecy, Qui-Gon determined to train Anakin in the ways of the Force.

Anakin left his mother on Tatooine and followed Qui-Gon to the capital of the Galactic Republic. After Qui-Gon's death at the hands of a Sith Lord, Anakin became the apprentice of another Jedi, Obi-Wan Kenobi.

Star Wars: Episode II—Attack of the Clones (2002)

Anakin Skywalker's skills increase—but so do the fear, anger, and impatience that will eventually lead to his downfall.

The Rise and Fall of Anakin Skywalker
Guided by Obi-Wan Kenobi, Anakin Skywalker rapidly rose to prominence among the Jedi. At the same time, something else

was rising—a dark rage within the fledgling Jedi's soul. Inescapable nightmares about his mother persistently haunted the boy. When Anakin had appeared before the Jedi Council, Master Yoda had warned, "Much fear in you, I sense, young one… Fear is the path to the dark side. Fear leads to anger, anger leads to hate, hate leads to suffering." Time would prove the truth of Yoda's observation.

While on an assignment to protect the beautiful senator Padmé Amidala Naberrie, Anakin returned to Tatooine to find his mother. He succeeded in his quest to locate his mother—but the cost to his soul was great. When he found his mother, she was dying. She had been abducted and mortally mauled by the savage Sand People. Surrendering to his inner rage, Anakin slaughtered the entire village of Sand People—not only warriors, but also women, children, and infants.

Star Wars: Episode III—Revenge of the Sith (2005)

At the end of an intragalactic civil war, Anakin Skywalker surrenders to the dark side of the Force and becomes Darth Vader, Dark Lord of the Sith.

The Last of the Jedi

Anakin sought solace in a secret marriage to Padmé, the senator from Naboo. Upon Anakin's return from the Clone Wars, Padmé revealed to Anakin that he would soon be a father.

Partly due to political upheavals in the Republic, Anakin also became the personal representative of Palpatine, a shrewd politician who had recently received far-reaching powers from the Galactic Senate. Everyone knew that Palpatine was a power-hungry opportunist. What few of them knew was that he was also a Sith Lord, the source of the imbalance in the Force.

By the time Anakin revealed the source of this elusive darkness to the Jedi High Council, Anakin had already fallen under Palpatine's spell. When Jedi Master Mace Windu attempted to arrest Palpatine, Anakin defended the dark emperor. Emperor Palpatine gave Anakin a fearsome new name—Darth Vader—and sent him on a vicious mission: Destroy the Jedi Order.

Anakin's murderous campaign against the Jedi culminated in a climactic duel with Obi-Wan Kenobi on the volcanic planet Mustafar. Believing that goodness still remained in Anakin, Obi-Wan tried to turn Anakin away from the dark side of the Force. Anakin rejected the redemption that Obi-Wan offered.

In the end, Obi-Wan Kenobi sent Anakin Skywalker hurtling into a pit of molten lava. Horribly mutilated and nearly dead, Anakin was rescued by Emperor Palpatine. The dark emperor equipped Anakin with prosthetic limbs and enshrouded him in terrifying black armor. In this way, Anakin Skywalker's transformation to the villainous Darth Vader, Dark Lord of the Sith, was complete.

In the aftermath of Anakin's surrender to the dark side of the Force, Padmé Amidala gave birth to twins, Leia and Luke. Knowing that the emperor would consider Anakin Skywalker's offspring to be a threat to his dark power, members of the burgeoning Rebel Alliance hid the infants. Anakin Skywalker's stepbrother, Owen Lars, became Luke's guardian on the planet Tatooine; Bail Organa, viceroy of the planet Alderaan, adopted Leia. Neither Owen nor Bail ever told the children about their father's true identity.

Following the deadly crusade that Emperor Palpatine and his new apprentice unleashed against the Jedi Order, only two

Jedi remained alive—Obi-Wan Kenobi and Yoda. Obi-Wan Kenobi vanished into the wastelands of Tatooine, and Yoda concealed himself in the swampy bogs of the planet Dagobah. Both Jedi awaited the moment when the ancient guardians of peace and justice could emerge anew, destroying Darth Vader and shattering the emperor's stranglehold on the galaxy.

Star Wars: Episode IV—A New Hope (1977)

Two decades after Anakin Skywalker's surrender to the dark side of the Force, his son, Luke, joins the rebellion against the Empire.

A New Jedi, a New Hope

During the intervening years, Leia became a senator from Alderaan and Luke grew into a restless farm boy, never satisfied with his lot at the present moment. Then an escape pod from a captured starship crash-landed in the sands of Tatooine. Two droids, R2–D2 and C–3P0, emerged from the pod and began a trek across the desert, eventually encountering Luke Skywalker. Somewhere within R2–D2's cantankerous circuits, the droid safeguarded detailed schematics from the emperor's massive battle station, the Death Star. It was essential that these plans made their way into the hands of the Rebel Alliance, so that they could destroy this new menace.

When Obi-Wan Kenobi encountered Luke and the two droids in the wastelands of Tatooine, the Jedi Knight recognized that it was time for Luke to understand the reason for his restless heart: Luke Skywalker was the son of a powerful Jedi, made for far more than Uncle Owen's moisture farm could ever provide. Still, Obi-Wan did not tell Luke the complete truth about his father: "A young Jedi named Darth Vader, who was a pupil of mine until he turned to evil, betrayed and murdered your father," Obi-Wan told Luke. "You must learn the ways of the Force if you're to come with me."

In this way, Luke, Obi-Wan, and two droids joined forces with the space pirate Han Solo and his woolly sidekick Chewbacca to deliver R2–D2 to representatives of the Rebel Alliance. After Imperial forces captured their ship, Obi-Wan faced his former pupil again.

"You can't win, Darth," Obi-Wan Kenobi vowed to Vader before forfeiting his own life so that his friends could escape. "If you strike me down, I shall become more powerful than you can possibly imagine"—and indeed he did. Despite the sacrifice of his body, Obi-Wan communed with Luke during the Battle of Yavin, enabling him to destroy the Death Star.

Star Wars: Episode V—The Empire Strikes Back (1980)

Darth Vader determines to draw his son into the dark side of the Force and, in the process, reveals that he is Luke's father.

Revelation

As Luke lay critically injured after an encounter with an alien beast, Obi-Wan appeared to Luke in a vision and instructed him to go to the planet Dagobah and seek out the Jedi Master Yoda, who would complete the young Jedi's training.

As Luke grew in his knowledge of the Force, Emperor Palpatine and Darth Vader devised a plan to lead Luke down the same path as his father. Luke's friends were used as bait to draw him into a duel with Darth Vader. There, Vader planned to entice Luke, luring him to the dark side of the Force.

At first, the ruse appeared to work. Ignoring Yoda's warnings, Luke left Dagobah before Yoda could complete his Jedi training. When he confronted the Sith Lord, Vader revealed the truth about Luke's parentage.

"Obi-Wan never told you what happened to your father," Vader said to Luke.

"He told me enough!" Luke screamed. "He told me you killed him."

"No," Darth Vader replied, "I am your father."

Still refusing to be seduced by the dark side of the Force, Luke escaped with the help of Leia.

Star Wars: Episode VI—Return of the Jedi (1983)

Darth Vader turns from the dark side of the Force and reclaims his true identity as Anakin Skywalker.

The Redemption of Anakin Skywalker
True to his word, Luke returned to Dagobah to complete his Jedi training. There he found Yoda close to death. Before passing away, Yoda confirmed the truth of Vader's words. "Your father he is."

As Luke prepared to leave Dagobah, the spirit of Obi-Wan Kenobi informed Luke that if he wanted to become a Jedi, one final task remained: "You must face Darth Vader again."

Luke protested, "I can't kill my own father."

"Then the Emperor has already won," Obi-Wan replied. "You were our only hope."

Despite Obi-Wan's admonitions, when Luke Skywalker faced Darth Vader again, he continued to believe that some goodness still remained in his father. Tempted not only by Vader but also by the Emperor, Luke nearly surrendered to his own inner rage—anger that would have lured him down the same dark path as his father. In the end, however, Luke chose the path of peace. Throwing his lightsaber aside, he said to the Emperor, "I'll never turn to the dark side. You've failed, Your Highness. I am a Jedi, like my father before me."

Unleashing a barrage of lightning, Emperor Palpatine would have killed Luke—but Palpatine discovered that a father's love could resist even the deepest darkness. On the threshold of death, Luke Skywalker looked to Darth Vader, crying out, "Father, please. Help me."

Confronted with his son's pleas, Darth Vader seized Emperor Palpatine and hurled him to his death. The darkness that had emerged decades earlier and burgeoned until it consumed the galaxy had finally been destroyed. The ancient prophecy of one who would bring balance to the Force had been fulfilled—but the fulfillment came at great cost.

Before falling to his death, Emperor Palpatine fatally injured Darth Vader. In Darth Vader's dying moments, he whispered to his son, "You were right. You were right about me. Tell your sister...you were right." Anakin Skywalker died in the arms of Luke Skywalker—the son who had refused to give up on his father and who, in the process, became his father's salvation.

A Serious Padawan's Guide to the Life of Awe

Suggestions for Group Study

The following outlines provide suggestions for interacting with this book in a small group. Before viewing any movies in your church or small group, secure the appropriate video license! You may obtain a license for a minimal charge at http://www.cvli.org.

Detailed outlines for eight sessions are provided here. If your group's curriculum is set up in a quarterly (thirteen-week) format, consider the following possibilities for five additional sessions:

1. Introductory Session

Plan an enjoyable, interactive introductory session. Before the session, provide a book, a name tag, and a three-by-five-inch card for each student. If possible, decorate your meeting area with *Star Wars* posters, and provide small *Star Wars* trinkets as door prizes. During the session:

(1) Have each person write on their card the name of the biblical character and the Star Wars character that they are most

like. Shuffle and redistribute the cards. Then ask each person to guess whose card she or he has.

(2) If your group members don't mind silliness, make up "Jedi names" for them. Here's one way to do it: After the first two or three letters of the person's first name, place a hyphen; then capitalize the next letter. If you want to be more creative, use last names too, separating them in odd places, to make them look like such names as Qui-Gon Jinn, Ki-Adi Mundi and Obi-Wan Kenobi. For example, someone named Amy Jo Ezell might become "Am-Yj Oezell." Dalton Franklin could be "Dal-Tonfran Klin." Hannah Jones might turn into "Han-Nahjo Nes." Use your "Jedi names" on your name tags!

(3) Review your expectations for the class with your students, encouraging them to read the Opening Credits and chapter 1 of the book before the next meeting.

(4) Pray together, asking God to guide your study.

2. "Not This Crude Matter"

The *Star Wars* films draw their ontology (view of reality) primarily from Eastern religions, such as Hinduism and Buddhism. In these religions, the physical world is perceived as evil or, more often, as *unreal*. For an example, look at the scene in *Episode V—The Empire Strikes Back* in which Yoda says to Luke, "Luminous beings are we…not this crude matter." In Eastern religions, salvation is ultimately an escape from "this crude matter." According to the Jewish and Christian Scriptures, however, God does not *rescue* His people from the material world; on the contrary, God's intention is to *redeem, restore,* and *reunite* every part of His creation, spiritual and material. Prepare a study that compares the biblical view of the material world with the view presented in *Star Wars*. For biblical references, see Romans 8:22–25 and 1 Corinthians 15:42–49.

3. *"It Is Your Destiny"*

Characters in the *Star Wars* films speak frequently about "destiny." For examples, look at the words spoken to Luke Skywalker by Obi-Wan Kenobi ("You cannot escape your destiny") and by Emperor Palpatine ("It is your destiny") in *Episode VI—Return of the Jedi*. Prepare a study that focuses on how our choices can change our destinies. Consider Ephesians 2:1–10 as a possible basis for this study. The opening verses of this text point out how and why humans are, by nature, destined for God's wrath. The remainder of the text makes it clear that this destiny may be changed through a personal choice that God initiates ("by grace," Ephesians 2:8; cf. 1:11–12) and humanity enacts ("through faith," Ephesians 2:8).

4. *"We Can Rule the Galaxy"*

Resisting temptation is a central motif in the *Star Wars* trilogies. For examples, see Darth Vader's attempt to lure Luke to the dark side in *Episode V—The Empire Strikes Back* ("Join me and we can rule the galaxy as father and son"), Palpatine's proposition to Anakin in *Episode III—Revenge of the Sith* ("Only through me can you achieve a power greater than any Jedi"), and Count Dooku's offer to Obi-Wan Kenobi in *Episode II—Attack of the Clones* ("Join me, Obi-Wan"). Compare one or more of these scenes with Satan's temptation of Jesus in Luke 4:1–13. How are the temptations similar? How are they different? Prepare a study that equips your students to resist temptations more effectively. Biblical references might include Mark 14:37–38, 66–72; 1 Corinthians 10:7–13; and Hebrews 4:14–16.

5. *Movie Time*

During the final session, enjoy one another's company as you watch a *Star Wars* film or play a *Star Wars* trivia game. Afterward, discuss the spiritual aspects of what you've experienced in this study. Don't forget the popcorn!

Session One

Every Journey Has a First Step

Learning Goal
Participants will understand that every aspect of their lives is extraordinary.

Look for Reflections of God's Story
Watch *Episode IV—A New Hope* from the appearance of the Twentieth-Century Fox logo to the stormtroopers' assault on the Rebel Blockade Runner. Ask the group, "What did you feel as you watched the video clip?" Draw out and focus on responses such as "Awe," "Wonder," and "Anticipation."

Listen to the Words of the Master
Read Ecclesiastes 3:11 aloud. Say, "There is, in every one of us, a longing to touch 'the forever' (NLV)—there is 'eternity in [our] hearts.' Those of you who felt awe and anticipation as you watched the movie's opening moments tasted a tiny glimmer of this inner longing. When, in your life, have you sensed the 'thoughts of the forever' (NLV) described in Ecclesiastes? When have you felt a sense of awe?"

Read Acts 2:43–47 aloud. Say, "It is God's desire that His

people not only long for awe but also live in awe. According to this text, the earliest believers' fellowship was an awe-inspiring experience. Have you ever experienced a sense of awe in the fellowship of believers? If so, describe your experience."

Some translations use "fear" in verse 43 instead of "awe." Be prepared to discuss the close relationship between awe and the fear of God. The fear of God is a natural outgrowth of authentic awe. This fear includes deep respect for God's character coupled with profound admiration of God's majesty. According to Scripture, the fear of God is an essential inclination of a healthy soul; it is a foundation of wisdom and a fountain of life (see Psalm 111:10; Proverbs 14:27; 19:23). This fear is not a curse to be avoided but a treasure to be pursued (see Isaiah 33:6).

Read Acts 17:26–28 aloud. Say, "When we fail to live in awe, it is usually because we have lost our awareness of God's presence. According to this text, however, every part of our lives is always permeated with God's presence. If this is true, nothing in our lives is ordinary, because an extraordinary God permeates every part of our lives! How can recognizing this fact change the way that we view the apparently ordinary events in our lives? How can this recognition help us to live in awe?"

Learn to Live in God's Story
Have your group complete the learning activity "Be Mindful of the True Force" located near the end of chapter 1. Discuss individual responses, as well as the reflection at the end of the chapter entitled "Meditate on the True Force." Then pray together. Before the group disperses, urge each student to read chapter 2 before the next session.

Session Two

"Your Eyes Can Deceive You"

Learning Goal
Participants will become aware of a larger world than their eyes can see.

Look for Reflections of God's Story
Watch the scene from *Star Wars: Episode IV—A New Hope* that's described in chapter 2. Ask the group, "What does taking 'your first step into a larger world' mean to you?"

Listen to the Words of the Master
Read 2 Corinthians 4:18 aloud. Say, "According to the book, 'In every moment of your life, a hidden realm—a vast world of wildness and wonder—surrounds you, gently caressing your innermost self.' This realm is what Paul seems to be talking about in this text. Describe a time when you clearly sensed this 'larger world.'"

Read Deuteronomy 28:65 aloud. Say, "When they were scattered among the nations, the Israelites lost their awareness of God's unseen presence among them. As a result, the people carried 'an anxious mind, eyes weary with longing, and a despairing heart.' What evidence do you see today that people around you have anxious minds, weary eyes, and despairing hearts? How might a deeper awareness of God's presence change these feelings?"

Read Philippians 4:8–12 aloud. Say, "In Philippians 4:8, Paul describes the essential qualities of experiences that reflect the larger world. Verse 12 describes the results of focusing our attention on this realm. How can people of our time center their lives on things that are true, honorable, right, pure, gracious, and admirable? How could this help us to become more contented?"

Learn to Live in God's Story
Have the group complete the learning activity "Be Mindful of the True Force" located at the end of chapter 2. Discuss individuals' responses, as well as the reflection at the end of the chapter entitled "Meditate on the True Force." Then pray together. Before the group disperses, urge each student to read chapter 3 before the next session.

Session Three

"That Is Why You Fail"

Learning Goal
Participants will begin to live "as if" the unseen world is the one that matters most.

Look for Reflections of God's Story
Watch the scene from *Star Wars: Episode V—The Empire Strikes Back* that's described in chapter 3. Say, "Believing means more than thinking that something is true. To have faith is to entrust yourself completely to something that you cannot see. It means learning to live in the power of the larger world. In light of this definition of faith, why did Luke Skywalker fail?"

You may need to point out that, in the original language of the New Testament, "faith" and "belief" are represented by the same Greek word.

Listen to the Words of the Master
Read Hebrews 11:1–16 aloud. Briefly summarize what it means to live "as if," according to chapter 3 of *Finding God in a Galaxy Far, Far Away*. Ask, "In what ways did the people mentioned in Hebrews 11 live 'as if' the unseen realm was the greatest reality

of all? Point out how the heroes and heroines of faith described in Hebrews 11 demonstrated their faith through their actions."

Read 2 Corinthians 5:6–7 aloud. Say, "To walk by faith is to focus our lives on this unseen realm. This does not necessarily mean thinking about heaven all the time. It means constantly recognizing God's living presence all around us, all the time. Name some practical ways that people today can live 'by faith, not by sight.'"

Learn to Live in God's Story
Have the group complete the learning activity "Be Mindful of the True Force" located near the end of chapter 3. Discuss individuals' responses, as well as the reflection at the end of the chapter entitled "Meditate on the True Force." Then pray together. Before the group disperses, urge each student to read chapter 4 before the next session.

Session Four

"Our Meeting Was Not a Coincidence"

Learning Goal
Participants will learn to stand in awe of God's presence in the lives of their fellow believers.

Look for Reflections of God's Story
Watch the scene from *Star Wars: Episode II—Attack of the Clones* that's described in chapter 4. Say, "Think about Palpatine's words to Anakin, 'You don't need guidance.' In what way did this suggestion lead Anakin toward the darkness?"

Listen to the Words of the Master
Read Genesis 1:26–28 and 2:18 aloud. Say, "To be created in God's image is to be created for fellowship—God is, after all, an infinite, intimate fellowship of Father, Son, and Spirit. Whenever we begin to believe that we don't need the guidance of others, we move toward the darker side of our human nature. In what ways do Christians today deny their need for guidance from other believers?"

Read 1 Corinthians 12:18–27 aloud. Say, "Many Christians in Corinth evidently assumed that they did not need the guidance of their fellow believers. Timothy Paul Jones refers to this assumption as 'the arrogant delusion that my salvation, my spiritual life, and my sins are personal matters.' How can you avoid this same 'arrogant delusion'?"

Read Acts 2:43–46 aloud. Say, "The Christians in Acts looked for God's presence in their fellowship with other believers; as a result, they were 'filled with awe' every day. In what specific ways can you imitate their example?"

Learn to Live in God's Story
Have the group complete the learning activity "Be Mindful of the True Force" located near the end of chapter 4. Discuss individuals' responses, as well as the reflection at the end of the chapter entitled "Meditate on the True Force." Then pray together. Before the group disperses, urge each student to read chapter 5 before the next session.

Session Five

"You Were My Brother"

Learning Goal
Participants will begin to imagine the presence of Jesus in every person who has a need.

Look for Reflections of God's Story
Watch the climactic scene in *Star Wars: Episode III—Revenge of the Sith* from Anakin's threat, "Don't make me destroy you, Master," to the words of Obi-Wan, "You were my brother, Anakin. I loved you." Ask the group, "What words might describe Obi-Wan Kenobi's feelings in this scene?" Draw out and focus on responses such as "betrayal" and "anger." Ask the group, "Why are Jedi Knights forbidden to give in to anger or to seek revenge?"

Listen to the Words of the Master
Read Leviticus 19:16–18 and Luke 6:27–31 aloud. Ask, "Why are God's people forbidden to seek revenge? In what ways are the commands of Jesus similar to what we read in Leviticus? In what ways do Jesus' words go beyond the commands of the Hebrew Scriptures?"

Read Matthew 25:31-46 aloud. Say, "According to Timothy Paul Jones, 'At its core, Christian faith is an exercise of the imagination... If I claim to follow Jesus Christ, God calls me to imagine the potential of His presence not only in the best and most beautiful...but also in the worst.' In light of Matthew 25:31–46, Jones encourages us to imagine the potential presence of Jesus in every person. How could this renewal of your imagination help you to forgive those who have wronged you?"

Learn to Live in God's Story
Have the group complete the learning activity "Be Mindful of the True Force" located near the end of chapter 5. Discuss individuals' responses, as well as the reflection at the end of the chapter entitled "Meditate on the True Force." Then pray together. Before the group disperses, urge each student to read chapter 6 before the next session.

Session Six

"Afraid, Are You?"

Learning Goal
Participants will learn to release to God everything that they fear to lose.

Look for Reflections of God's Story
Watch the scene from *Star Wars: Episode I—The Phantom Menace* that's described at the beginning of chapter 6. Say, "According to Timothy Paul Jones, 'Fear arises when we realize that we are not in control—and, deep inside, each of us longs to be in control.' In what ways does this statement describe Anakin Skywalker as he stands before the Jedi Council? What about later, in Episodes II and III?

Listen to the Words of the Master
Read Genesis 3:1–10 aloud. Say, "The desire of the first humans to be in control (see vv. 4–6) led to fear (see v. 10). Fear led to anger (see vv. 11–13), hate (see Genesis 4:8), and suffering (see Genesis 3:16–19; 4:10–16). Describe a situation in your life in which your desire to be in control led to fear, anger, hate, or suffering."

Read Matthew 6:25–34 and Luke 14:25–27 aloud. Say, "These passages describe God's solution to the problem of fear: Release to God everything you fear to lose. In Matthew 6, Jesus commands His followers to release their desire to be in control of their clothing, food, and drink. In Luke 14, the requirement goes even deeper, expanding to include our families and even our own lives."

Be prepared to discuss the command to "hate" one's family. For a brief discussion of this phrase, see the IVP New Testament commentaries at www.biblegateway.com/resources/commentaries. For a more detailed discussion, see O. Michel, "miseo," *Theological Dictionary of the New Testament*, vol. 4, ed. Gerhard Kittel (Grand Rapids, MI: William B. Eerdmans, 1967), 683–94.

Say, "Now let's look at Yoda's solution to the problem of fear." Watch the scene in *Star Wars: Episode III—Revenge of the Sith* in which Anakin Skywalker goes to Yoda for advice. Begin with Yoda's words, "Premonitions… Hmmmm." Stop as Anakin hurries down the temple hallway. Ask the group, "How are Yoda's words similar to the command of Jesus? What is different about Yoda's suggestion?"

Read Isaiah 43:1–7 aloud. Say, "This passage tells us why we can let go of everything we fear to lose—because God has promised to be with us in every circumstance (see vv. 1–2, 5). When we refuse to entrust ourselves and our fears to God, we are not living as if God is always with us. How can this passage encourage you to release everything to God throughout this week?"

Learn to Live in God's Story
Have the group complete the learning activity "Be Mindful of the True Force" located near the end of chapter 6. Discuss individuals' responses, as well as the reflection at the end of the

chapter entitled "Meditate on the True Force." Then pray together. Before the group disperses, urge each student to read chapter 7 before the next session.

"When You Are Calm, at Peace"

Learning Goal

Participants will learn to live in peace by letting go of their shadows.

Look for Reflections of God's Story

Watch the scene from *Star Wars: Episode V—The Empire Strikes Back* that's described at the beginning of chapter 7. Ask, "Why does Luke Skywalker see his own face in Darth Vader's helmet?" After several responses, guide students toward these words from the book: "Crawling into the darkness with his hand resting on his weapons, Luke takes his own inner chaos with him. When he sees his own face in Darth Vader's helmet, he learns that the one he is destroying with his lack of peace isn't the Dark Lord of the Sith; it is himself. Before Luke can defeat the darkness of his enemy, he must first confront the shadows in himself. So must you."

Listen to the Words of the Master

Read John 14:27 aloud. Say, "God's plan is for His people to live in peace. Do most Christians constantly experience God's peace?

Why or why not? How do our 'shadows,' as described in this chapter, keep us from the full experience of divine peace?"

Say, "Describe some 'shadows' that keep people from experiencing God's peace." Read aloud Isaiah 53:4–6. Say, "On the cross, Jesus carried not only our sins ('iniquity,' v. 6) but also our shadows ('infirmities,' 'sorrows,' v. 4). His purpose in this was to bring us 'peace' (v. 5). That's why we can release our shadows to Jesus—He has already carried them!"

Say, "When we release our shadows to God's power, we experience a peace that's greater than human comprehension. Paul described this sort of peace in his letter to Philippi." Read aloud Philippians 4:4–9. Say, "In light of this text, what specific attitudes or actions could you change during this week?"

Learn to Live in God's Story
Have the group complete the learning activity "Be Mindful of the True Force" located near the end of chapter 7. Discuss individuals' responses, as well as the reflection at the end of the chapter entitled "Meditate on the True Force." Then pray together. Before the group disperses, urge each student to read chapter 8 and the Closing Credits before the next session.

Session Eight

Epic Possibilities in Unexpected Places

Learning Goal
Participants will begin to notice the epic possibilities that already fill every part of their lives.

Look for Reflections of God's Story
Watch the climactic scene in *Star Wars: Episode VI—Return of the Jedi* from Darth Vader's words to Luke Skywalker, "Obi-Wan's failure is complete," to the death of Anakin Skywalker. Ask the group, "What did Luke Skywalker see when he looked at Darth Vader? What did everyone else see? How was Luke able to see epic possibility in the arch villain of the galaxy?"

Listen to the Words of the Master
Organize the class into five groups. Assign each group one of the following Scriptures: *Group 1:* 1 Samuel 16:1–18:7; *Group 2:* Matthew 6:26–34; *Group 3:* Luke 2:1–7; *Group 4:* John 4:1–42; *Group 5:* John 7:53–8:11. Encourage the participants in each group to survey their text together. When you have reassembled, ask each group the following questions:

Group 1: What did David's brothers see in David? What did God see in him?

Group 2: What did other people see when they looked at the lilies and the birds? What did Jesus see?

Group 3: What would casual observers have thought when they saw a baby in a feed trough? What did the angels see?

Group 4: What did the disciples and the townspeople see when they looked at the Samaritan woman? What did Jesus see?

Group 5: What did the religious leaders see in this woman? What did Jesus see?

Read 1 Corinthians 1:25–29 aloud. Say, "In God's story—as in the finest of the fairy tales—the most crucial people and objects are the ones that seem worthless and weak. That's because God sees epic possibilities where others see only difficulties. How can you look for epic possibilities in the people and circumstances that you will encounter this week?"

Learn to Live in God's Story

Have the group complete the learning activity "Be Mindful of the True Force" located near the end of chapter 8. Discuss their responses, as well as the reflection at the end of the chapter entitled "Meditate on the True Force." Then pray together.

Bibliography

Bouzereau, Laurent, ed. *The Annotated Screenplays: Star Wars, Episodes IV–VI*. New York: Random House, 1997.

Bresman, Jonathan. *The Art of Star Wars: Episode I—The Phantom Menace*. New York: Del Rey, 1999.

Brooks, Terry. *Star Wars, Episode I—The Phantom Menace*. New York: Del Rey, 1999.

Lucas, George. *Star Wars: Episode III—Revenge of the Sith: The Illustrated Screenplay and The Final Chapter*. Adobe Reader® E-Book. New York: Del Rey, 2005.

Salvatore, R. A. *Star Wars: Episode II—Attack of the Clones*. New York: Del Rey, 2002.

Stover, Matthew. *Star Wars: Episode III—Revenge of the Sith*. New York: Del Rey, 2005.

Vaz, Mark Cotta. *The Art of Star Wars: Episode II—Attack of the Clones*. New York: Del Rey, 2002.

Endnotes

Chapter One

1. Quoted in Daniel Kennelly, "Longing for Eden," *Crisis* (June 1999): 41–43.

2. George Lucas with Bill Moyers, "Of Myth and Men," *Time* (April 26, 1999): 92–93.

3. The foundations of this inner longing are, it seems, analogous to C. G. Jung's concept of "the collective unconscious." See "The Concept of the Collective Unconscious" in *The Portable Jung* (New York: Viking, 1971), 60–61. Jung, unfortunately, traced the foundations of the collective unconscious only as far as a series of universal archetypes, failing to recognize that the collective unconscious has its basis in humanity's creation in the image of an intracommunal deity (see Genesis 1:26–28) in whom the archetypal longings may be satisfied.

4. Rudolf Otto, *Das Heilige* (Breslau: Trewendt und Granier, 1923), 13–14. The *mysterium* seems to be the foundation of the human reaction to divine majesty described so eloquently by John Calvin: "Thus, there is that dread and awe which Scripture consistently relates, with which saints were struck and overwhelmed whenever they glimpsed God's presence." See John Calvin, *Institutio Christianae religionis,* in *Ioannis Calvini opera selecta* (Munich: Christliche Kaiser, 1926), 1:1:3.

5. William James, *The Varieties of Religious Experience* (New York: Mentor, 1902), 61–62.

6. The phenomenon to which I refer as "awe" is analogous to "the awareness of absolute dependence" (*das schlechthinnigen Abhängigkeitsgefuehl*) in Friedrich D.E. Schleiermacher's theology, as well as the structural-developmental phenomenon variously described as "other-awareness," "spiritual transcendence," and "relational consciousness." See D. Hay and R. Nye, *Spirit of the Child* (Loveland, CO: Fount, 1998), 10; Timothy Paul Jones,

"James W. Fowler's Stages of Faith and Friedrich Schleiermacher's *Gefuehl* as Spiritual Transcendence," *Midwestern Journal of Theology* (Spring 2005): 59–71; F. D. E. Schleiermacher, *Die christliche Sitte nach den Grundsätzen der evangelischen Kirche im Zusammenhang dargestellt* (Berlin: Reimer, 1843), 3:3; 5:1–3; 33:1; 34:1. Although James W. Fowler has referred to this phenomenon as "faith," it differs from Christian faith at the most fundamental level. It is more properly understood as a contextual foundation of faith, *out of which* faith grows but *from which* faith remains distinct. See also Timothy Paul Jones, *An Analysis of the Relationship Between Fowlerian Stage-Development and Self-Assessed Maturity in Christian Faithfulness Among Evangelical Christians* (Louisville, KY: The Southern Baptist Theological Seminary, 2003), 35–37.

7. Augustine was describing one aspect of awe when he wrote, "*Quid est illud quod interlucet mihi et percutit cor meum sine laesione? et inhorresco et inardesco: inhorresco, in quantum dissimilis ei sum, inardesco, in quantum similis ei sum*" ("What is it that shines through me, and strikes my heart without hurting it? I quake in awe and burn with its fire! I shudder, because I am unlike it; I burn with fire, because it is unlike me.") Augustine, *Confessiones*, 11:9:11. Augustine later identified the object of this description as "wisdom." For an identification of *wisdom* with the phenomenon referred to above as *spiritual transcendence,* see Jones, *An Analysis,* 152–54.

8. S. M. Ulam, *Adventures of a Mathematician* (New York: Scribners, 1976), 289.

9. G. K. Chesterton, *Orthodoxy,* www.ccel.org/c/chesterton/orthodoxy.html.

10. Leonard Sweet, *SoulSalsa: 17 Surprising Steps for Godly Living in the 21st Century* (Grand Rapids, MI: Zondervan, 2000), 31.

11. Ken Gire, "Faithful Companions and Guides: Art and Nature as God's Chosen Vocabulary," *Mars Hill Review* (Fall 1996): 8–20.

12. Lucas with Moyers, "Of Myth and Men," 92.

Part I

1. Brennan Manning, *The Ragamuffin Gospel* (Sisters, OR: Multnomah, 1990), 88–89.

Chapter Two

1. "Domine…quia fecisti nos ad te et inquietum est cor nostrum, donec requiescat in te" (Augustine, *Confessiones,* 1:1:1).

2. J. R. R. Tolkien, *The Lord of the Rings* (New York: Houghton Mifflin, 1994), 42.

3. C. S. Lewis, *Mere Christianity* (New York: Harper, 1952), 136–37.

4. Chesterton, *Orthodoxy*

5. Jürgen Moltmann and Hans Küng have contended that, although the unseen realm may be experienced in the present, its reality is in the future. See Küng, *On Being a Christian* (Garden City, NY: Doubleday, 1976), 220–224. See also Moltmann, *Theology of Hope: On the Ground and the Implications of a Christian Eschatology* (Minneapolis: Fortress Press, 1993), 202. I suggest that the unseen realm is a fully present reality, veiled from our present view by our own limited perceptions. See, for example, D. R. Griffin, *God and Religion in a Postmodern World* (Albany, NY: State University of New York, 1989), 105. Although we cannot change the limitations of our terrestrial perceptions, we can learn to live every present moment fully aware of this larger, unseen reality around us.

6. T. S. Eliot, "The Modern Dilemma," *The Christian Register*, October 19, 1933. Quoted in Philip Yancey, *Rumors of Another World* (Grand Rapids, MI: Zondervan, 2003), 177.

7. C. S. Lewis, *The Great Divorce* (New York: Harper, 1946), 69–70.

8. Elizabeth Barrett Browning, *Aurora Leigh, book vii,* http://www.bartleby.com/100/446.23.html.

9. Frederick Buechner, *The Hungering Dark* (New York: HarperCollins, 1969), 13.

10. G. K. Chesterton, from "A Defense Against Defending Things," the introduction to his 1914 book *The Defendant,* www.cornerstonemag.com/imaginarium/inklinks/.

Chapter Three

1. "Et aliud est de silvestri cacumine videre patriam pacis…et aliud tenere viam illuc ducentem," (Augustine of Hippo, *Confessiones,* 7:21:27).

2. Translated from John Calvin, *Institutio Christianae religionis,*
   3:2:36. Karl Barth makes much the same point with his concept
   of Bekennen, the aspect of faith that personally commits the
   individual to Jesus Christ and shatters any illusion of self-
   determination. See Karl Barth, *Die kirchliche Dogmatik* (Zurich,
   Switzerland: Evangelische Verlag, 1936–1962) 4:1:767–79.
3. Summarized from Timothy Paul Jones, "The Necessity of
   Objective Assent in the Act of Christian Faith," *Bibliotheca Sacra*
   (April–June 2005).
4. Hans-Jürgen Hermission and Eduard Lohse, *Faith* (Nashville,
   TN: Abingdon, 1978), 168.
5. Quoted in Sweet, *SoulSalsa,* 127.
6. Some biblical scholars understand this text to refer to a primeval
   event in which Jesus saw Satan cast from heaven when he
   rebelled against God; however, the imperfect tense of the verb
   implies an event that, from Jesus' perspective, began in the
   recent past and was ongoing. See Craig Keener, *The IVP Bible
   Background Commentary* (Downers Grove, IL: InterVarsity, 1993),
   217; John Nolland, *Luke 9:21–18:34* (Dallas, TX: Word, 1993),
   563–64.
7. Terri Windling, "White as Snow," in *Snow White, Blood Red* (New
   York: Eos, 1993), 1–15.

Part II
1. J. R. R. Tolkien, *The Lord of the Rings* (New York: Houghton
   Mifflin, 1994), 697.

Chapter Four
1. William Willimon and Stanley Hauerwas, *Lord, Teach Us: The
   Lord's Prayer and the Christian Life* (Nashville, TN: Abingdon,
   1996), 28.
2. Language alludes to Paul Tournier, quoted in Philip Yancey,
   Church: Why Bother? (Grand Rapids, MI: Zondervan, 1998), 37.
3. C. S. Lewis, *The Weight of Glory: And Other Addresses* (New York:
   Harper, 1949), 46.
4. Dietrich Bonhoeffer, *Life Together* (New York: Harper, 1954), 78.

Chapter Five

1. Some dialogue in this chapter appeared in the original screenplay of *Star Wars: Episode III—Revenge of the Sith* but was cut from the final film.
2. Frederick Buechner, *Wishful Thinking: A Seeker's ABC* (New York: Harper, 1993), 2.
3. Frederick Buechner, *The Hungering Dark* (New York: HarperSanFrancisco, 1985), 14.
4. Quoted in Mark Buchanan, *Your God Is Too Safe* (Sisters, OR: Multnomah), 53.
5. Another example of this phenomenon may be found in *The Lord of the Rings*. The only clause that recurs in all three installments of the trilogy is "The pity of Bilbo [in sparing Gollum's life] may rule the fate of many." Gandalf represents the sort of "imagination" that I have described here when he says to Frodo, "My heart tells me that he has some part to play yet, for good or ill, before the end; and when that comes, the pity of Bilbo may rule the fate of many—yours not least" (Tolkien, *The Lord of the Rings,* 68–69).
6. The use of the concept of "imagination" in this chapter was inspired by the phrase "the baptized imagination" in expositions of C. S. Lewis's writings. For an exploration of this motif, see Ralph C. Wood, "The Baptized Imagination: C.S. Lewis's Fictional Apologetics," *The Christian Century* (August 30, 1995): 812–15.
7. Willimon and Hauerwas, *Lord, Teach Us*, 79–86.

Part III

1. J. R. R. Tolkien, "On Fairy Stories," *The Tolkien Reader,* ed. P. S. Beagle (New York: Ballantine, 1966, 1986), 67–69.
2. J. R. R. Tolkien, *The Letters of J. R. R. Tolkien,* eds. Humphrey Carpenter and Christopher Tolkien (Boston: Houghton Mifflin, 1981), letter 89.
3. Tolkien, "On Fairy Stories," 69.

Chapter Six

1. Quoted in Grant Martin, *Transformed by Thorns* (Wheaton, IL: Victor, 1985), 95–96.

2. The fear described in this chapter should be clearly distinguished from *the fear of God*. Fear of God is a natural outgrowth of authentic wonder and awe. This fear includes deep respect for God's character coupled with profound admiration of God's majesty. According to Scripture, the fear of God is an essential inclination of a healthy soul; it is a foundation of wisdom and a fountain of life (see Psalm 111:10; Proverbs 14:27; 19:23). This fear is not a curse to be avoided but a treasure to be pursued (see Isaiah 33:6).

3. Stanislav Grof contends that fear is the first emotion that an infant experiences. See *Spiritual Emergency: When Personal Transformation Becomes a Crisis* (New York: Putnam, 1989), 8–12. For a brief summary of Grof's research, see Joseph Campbell with Bill Moyers, *The Power of Myth* (New York: Anchor, 1988), 59.

4. "En messôi d'adamantos eên Phobos ou ti phateios," Hesiod, "The Shield of Heracles," in *Loeb Classical Library, Volume 57: Hesiod, Homeric Hymns, Epic Cycle, Homerica* (Cambridge, MA: Harvard, 1981), sections 139–40.

5. C. S. Lewis, *The Last Battle* (New York: HarperCollins, 1956, 1984), 69.

6. Jakob Grimm, et al., "Märchen von einem, der auszog, das Fürchten zu lernen," in *Kinder- und Hausmarchen* (Ditzingen, Germany: Reclam, 2001).

7. The Greek text of Luke 14:26 reads "hate" (*misein*) rather than "let go." "Hate" is, however, used in this context to indicate a person or path that is not chosen. See, for example., F. F. Bruce, *The Hard Sayings of Jesus* (Downers Grove, IL: InterVarsity, 1983), 120; Walter C. Kaiser Jr., *Toward Old Testament Ethics* (Grand Rapids, MI: Zondervan, 1983), 252. As such, "let go" accurately renders the original intent of the text.

8. Paraphrased from Matthew 5:42 and Luke 6:30.

9. Language alludes to Brennan Manning, *Lion and Lamb: The Relentless Tenderness of Jesus* (Grand Rapids, MI: Chosen, 1986), 58, 90.

10. Adapted from George MacDonald, "The Sacred Present," in *George MacDonald: Anthology,* ed. C. S. Lewis (New York: HarperCollins, 2001), 39.

Chapter Seven

1. C. G. Jung described this mythological motif as the Shadow Archetype. "By overcoming the dark passions"—Campbell's term for humanity's *shadow side*—"the hero symbolizes our ability to control the irrational savage within us." See Campbell with Moyers, *The Power of Myth*, xiii; C. G. Jung, *The Archetypes and the Collective Unconscious*, ed. R. F. C. Hull (Princeton, NJ: Princeton University, 1969), 20–21, 285, 322; C. G. Jung, *Letters,* ed. G. Adler (Princeton, NJ: Princeton University, 1973), 234. For an analysis of another modern myth from the perspective of Jung's archetypes, see Pia Skogemann's excellent *En jungiansk fortolkning af Tolkiens Ringenes Herre* (Copenhagen, Denmark: Athene, 2004).

2. Jody G. Bower, "*The Lord of the Rings*—An Archetypical Hero's Journey," http://greenbooks.theonering.net/guest/files/120101_02.html/

3. Henri J. M. Nouwen, *The Wounded Healer* (New York: Doubleday, 1979), 93.

Chapter Eight

1. Campbell with Moyers, *The Power of Myth*, 44.

2. J. R. R. Tolkien, "On Fairy Stories," 67–69.

3. Language alludes to C. S. Lewis, *The Weight of Glory,* 31.

4. Quoted in Daniel Kennelly, "Longing for Eden," 41–43.

5. C. S. Lewis, *God in the Dock: Essays on Theology and Ethics* (Grand Rapids, MI: Eerdmans, 1970), 66–67.

6. Leonard Sweet, *Postmodern Pilgrims: First-Century Passion for the Twenty-first-Century Church* (Nashville, TN: Broadman, 2000), 86

7. G. K. Chesterton, "The Priest of Spring," in *A Miscellany of Men* (New York: Dodd, 1912), 112.

8. Tolkien, "On Fairy Stories," 69.

9. Frederick Buechner, *Whistling in the Dark: A Doubter's Dictionary* (New York: HarperCollins, 1988), 73.

10. Leonard Sweet, *Out of the Question…Into the Mystery: Getting Lost in the GodLife Relationship* (New York: Waterbrook, 2004), 199.

11. Translated from John Chrysostom, "Continens homilias in epistolam ad Corinthios priorem, Oxonii," in *Sancti patris nostri Ioannis chrysostomi archiepiskopou Constantinopolitani interpretatio*

omnium epistolarum Paulinarum per homilias facta vol. 2, ed. F. Field (Paris: Apud Gulielmum Merlin, 1847), homily 21.

12. C. S. Lewis, *The Last Battle* (New York: HarperCollins, 1956), 228.

13. J. R. R. Tolkien, *The Lord of the Rings*, 72.

The Closing Credits

1. Roger Ebert, "*Star Wars* (1977)," http://rogerebert.suntimes.com/.

2. Roger Ebert, "*Star Wars: Episode I—The Phantom Menace*," http://rogerebert.suntimes.com/.

3. Ibid.

STAR WARS FANS!

Coming to a DVD Player Near You

Win the ultimate *Star Wars* DVD collection! This prize package contains the original Star Wars Trilogy four-disc DVD set and two-disc special editions of *Episode 1: The Phantom Menace, Episode II: Attack of the Clones*, and the newly released *Episode III: Revenge of the Sith*—a retail value of more than $139. All DVDs are widescreen editions and include a galaxy of extras!

Log on to **www.revelinwonder.com** to sign up for your chance to win one of four complete sets. All entries must be received by December 15, 2005.

Multnomah® Publishers   *Keeping Your Trust…One Book at a Time*®